CRAPS

TO PLAY LIKE A PRO
LEARN FROM A PRO

by

Sam Grafstein

"The Dice Doctor"

This edition published by
ATLANTIC CITY NEWS, PACIFIC & ILLINOIS AVE., ATLANTIC CITY, NEW JERSEY

CRAPS

TO PLAY LIKE A PRO
LEARN FROM A PRO

by

Sam Grafstein

"The Dice Doctor"

CONTENTS

PREFACE

The following pages contain an honest and helpful collection of plays and pieces of advice for the crapshooter that wants to PLAY FOR KEEPS.

You won't find any (chase your money) sucker systems in this book. In detail and CORRECTLY we will describe for both the RIGHT and the WRONG bettors, all of the most popular plays. Dollar-wise, this amounts to more than 80% of ALL crap table play. (In legal casinos as well as illegal floating crap games.)

The other 15 or 20% of the crap table plays?? We won't waste too much space or time on them. They include the CHASE YOUR LOSSES SYSTEMS . . . the MORE EXPENSIVE house edge bets, plus a few others that I choose to call IDIOT BETS. We will touch very lightly on some of these bets and should any of them be your choice of bets, then I will teach you how to play them like an INTELLIGENT IDIOT.

In my more than 60 years as a bettor, as a bookie (crap game employee), as well as a craps game teacher, I believe that in one form or another, I've pretty well seen all of the plays.

When working with a crapshooter, I don't tell him (or her) what plays to make. That choice I leave to the player. I can and do however, show the player the BEST WAY in which he can make his play. In other words: HOW TO PLAY FOR KEEPS.

I won't guarantee that you will consistently beat the MINUS FACTOR or HOUSE EDGE of the casino, or any other bank craps type of game. What I will guarantee, is that should anything in the way of a hand or shoot show, "YOU WILL GET THE MONEY". ("Getting the money" in street talk, means to wind up with many times more in winnings, than the average player will win on the SAME hand or shoot, starting with the SAME initial bet.)

At the very least, you will become as good as, or better than, any crapshooter at the table.

HUMAN NATURE IS THE GAMBLER'S WORST ENEMY,
THE HOUSE EDGE IS A PIKER IN COMPARISON.

Sam Grafstein
"The Dice Doctor"

INTRODUCTION

How much would you charge for an hour or two of your time?? One hundred dollars? One thousand dollars? One hundred thousand dollars? Don't laugh!! This was not meant to sound absurd or sarcastic. The time required to read these pages, could dollar-wise be worth as much or more. (For your nerves and mental well-being, even more than the money.)

MAN HAS ALWAYS GAMBLED

HE GAMBLES NOW

HE WILL ALWAYS GAMBLE

In your business or profession, you would normally research and prepare before investing your money. Why wouldn't you do the same before you invest at the GAMING TABLES?? It's the same money isn't it? Or is it?? Perhaps it's a rich wife's inheritance, or a piece of the boss' money you forgot to place into the till? Watch the play of MOST gamblers. You'll swear they can't be using money they had to WORK for.

The amount of reading and preparation time required is negligible, compared to the amount YOU MAY SAVE IN LOSSES when you lose, or the amount YOU MAY GAIN IN WINNINGS when you win.

I DON'T ADVOCATE GAMBLING!! But if you do gamble ... PLAY FOR KEEPS. To say you are PLAYING FOR FUN, when money or materials are the stakes, IS AN INSULT TO THE INTELLIGENCE OF A RETARDED INBECILE!!

Occasional players (unlike those of us that have 365 days of the year in which to play) have limited time and find it difficult to accept the patience required, as one of the first gambling rules towards becoming the successful player. He feels that HE MUST TAKE SHOTS This lack of patience also prevents the player from accepting that today's game is a continuation of yesterday's game. That tomorrow's game (tomorrow actually, or a year from tomorrow literally) is an extension of today's game.

Put simply, gambling is a continuous game. It lasts for your lifetime. Taking that ONE LAST SHOT is another SICK MOVE. Taking that last shot to try getting even at a stag, a floating crap game or a junket, leads to a worse letdown than a dozen losses while you are in regular action. Even a net winner gets depressed on a LAST SHOT LOSS. (Yes, I agree it's possible to win on that last shot!! But is it really worth it??)

Most players that are FINANCIALLY PRECISE in their own line of business or profession, become an UNDISCIPLINED BUNCH OF INFANTILE IDIOTS, when they reach the gaming tables. (I hope the wording IDIOT BETTOR, won't take too long to sink in.)

Although the casino caters to every whim and fancy of the weak player, (even 38-26-38) behind their backs (if the shoe fits, wear it) THEY LAUGH ALL THE WAY TO THE BANK!! (I wish I had originated that quote.)

In case you think I'm being sarcastic, you're right!! Show me that you've reached some maturity in your play at the gaming tables, and I'll not only respect you for it, but I'll lay a price that you are a MATURE person away from the gaming tables.

Don't try impressing the casino personnel with your LOSSES. They will respect you much more as a WINNER. (Comp-wise and otherwise.) These casino people also have friends and families to go home to. The LAST thing they care to take home with them are LOSER stories. Many of these casino people had gone the loser route themselves, before reaching their own maturity. (If they were lucky.)

Many players are truly liked and respected by the casino personnel. They are not necessarily the hi-rollers, but they do have that extra bit of class. Granted, the casino (for "bottom line" reasons) is obligated to cater to the hi-roller, but there is nothing in the book that says you must like them. You do have to earn their respect, the same as you would away from the casino. The choice is all yours!!

There are a small minority of gamblers who have sucessfully met the challenge of the House Edge. No!! They haven't come up with a magic formula for changing the MINUS FACTOR against the player, to a PLUS FACTOR in favor of the player. Members of this minority have served their apprenticeship and PAID THEIR DUES.

MONEY MANAGEMENT, PATIENCE and SENSIBLE PROGRESSIVE BETTING, now comes automatically to them. This LIMITED group can go into any casino anywhere in the world, with serious money in their pockets. They are not in the least bit worried that they "WILL TAKE THE STEAM." (Chase their losses if the dice should go against them.)

These players have learned how to put a PREDETERMINED LIMIT on their LOSSES. At the same time, they will NEVER LIMIT THEIR WINNINGS. (These players will walk away with the crap table AND the casino, if the dice should go their way. They don't know what it means to feel sorry for the House.)

It is this player who can take his wife or girl friend (the opposite in the case of the woman gambler) to the best shows and finest gourmet restaurants. Not as a duty, but as a genuine pleasure for some of the finer extras in life. He didn't get anything for nothing. He worked for, earned, and now deserves these extras.

These players, having reached maturity at the gaming tables, can now afford the luxury of being a nice guy, and helpful to his fellow gambler. It took me more than 50 years of apprenticeship and practice, plus lots of money and mental cost, to reach this MATURITY at the crap table. The first 30 years were disastrous!! The past 20 years?? Not too bad. I now like my chances, despite the House Edge. I've even gotten to like myself, for my changed outlook on gambling and life in general. LIFE AND GAMBLING HAVE MORE THAN MUCH IN COMMON.

According to rule, the rolls of the dice should be a win, a loss. A win, a loss. They are in the long run meant to average out to where both the Right AND the Wrong Bettor gets chopped up. Were these end results to be accepted by us crapshooters, then we would just return to playing with marbles. Fortunately for us, the long run average applies to EVERY crap game EVERYWHERES in the world.

So, what are WE looking and hoping for? For the Right Bettor, he hopes that either he or another shooter he is betting on, will roll a small or big PROFIT HAND. Or just maybe the exception---A REAL MONSTER OF A HAND!

On the other hand, the Wrong or Backline Bettor hopes that the dice will go around the table a couple of times, without ANY shooter making a pass.

We as crapshooters should care very little about the MATHEMATICAL END RESULTS. As a Right or as a Wrong bettor, should the dice turn in our direction, WE'LL KNOW EXACTLY HOW TO TAKE FULL ADVANTAGE. (That's why this book was put into print.)

The really big hands or shoots during the lifetime of the crapshooter are memorable events. These hands are vivid in the minds of the crapshooter 10, 15 and even 20 or more years after they've taken place. Most of the post mortems and tall stories take place after these hands or shoots are history.

How many times haven't you heard a crapshooter complain as to how many thousands, instead of hundreds he could have won, had he only given HIS GAMBLING MONEY a FAIR GAMBLE. (It's money that was earmarked for gambling. What are you waiting for??)

As for stories. Crapshooters will swear on a stack that the 25 minute hand, lasted an hour and 15 minutes. The crap table crew and the pit personnel are no slouches either, when it comes to stretching the time that a hand was in action. Just ask any of them how long the last 12 minute hand lasted? Without blinking an eyelash, they'll say 45 minutes!! Of course, they forget to mention that the 45 minutes included the rolls of the last 17 shooters. (9 of which were consecutive miss-outs.) All kidding aside, dealers and pit personnel are not liars. (They are just trained to make sales.) PREVARICATE A BIT IF NECESSARY.)

In 1933, at the Chicago World's Fair, I worked as a "paper dealer" (just cash, no chips) in one of the many floating crap games, in and around the Fair Grounds. I was "on stick" this one night and called what for me was to be a personal record. I called a 23 pass hand, which included only 4 Naturals (7-11) at the RIGHT TIME, (right time meaning that they showed on the come-out roll for a new pass-line point) plus 19 Pass Line points, and not ONE crap roll on the come-out roll for a new Pass Line Point.

After calling the fourth or fifth pass, my boss ordered me off the stick. (Unlike casino stickmen who are on stick for a set period of time, during which time they could call 2 or even 22 passes by the same shooter and not get called off the stick. In floating crap games, the boss can call you off the stick after ONE pass or even too many box numbers.)

Not too long ago at a floating crap game in Toronto, the boss had three stickmen on for this one shooter. This shooter hadn't even made his FIRST pass, but he was rolling a bunch of numbers. Finally the boss himself took the stick, and after a couple of rolls, called the miss-out. (A real MICKEY MOUSE MOVE by the House. NO CLASS!!)

Getting back to this "MONSTER" of a hand. Unfortunately, (for the boss) there were a few "boys" in the game with bulges under their jackets. They made it clear that I was to finish calling the hand. After about the 14th or 15th pass, my boss called it an UNFINISHED HAND, as he was now tapped out. (Broke.)

The rackets gentlemen wouldn't even take that for an answer. They insisted I finish calling the hand, and that they would take my boss' PERSONAL MARKERS if they should beat him for more.

Since he had nothing further to lose, he agreed. He also knew if he had refused, that things could get a little messy. Cement was quite reasonable at that time. I'm just kidding. They didn't use cement. (They used PIG IRON.)

These gentlemen knew that my boss was above all an honorable man, and would if he got stuck in for more, eventually pay off his I.O.U.'s or markers, 100 cents on the dollar. Besides, one of the "boys" was the shooter putting on the hand. His egotism dictated that he continue putting on the show, in spite of his having broke the House. (I had learned very early, that honoring another operator's markers was a common courtesy, providing his past performances warranted it. It was also a known fact that these crap game operators would have no trouble getting bankrolled for the following night's game. Especially if he ran a liked game with a good following.)

The shortstops and desperados were not permitted to play any longer in this

MARKER CRAP GAME. (They had all they wanted anyways.)

I was fired for calling this hand. It was a good thing for the dealers that we were dealing in paper (money) and not in chips. Otherwise, instead of winding up with some serious money in tokes, we could have wound up waiting for our night's wages. I bought a piece of this game a few days later. THIS boss would never again let me go on stick. (I wonder why??)

After the gambler reaches his maturity at the gaming tables, he can make one of three decisions:

(1) Make gambling a full-time job.

(2) Make gambling his leisure-time hobby.

(3) Give up gambling altogether.

On decisions (1) and (2), I wish you luck and an understanding wife and family. On decision (3), I can and will guarantee that you will be FAR AHEAD of the most successful gambler who ever lived. What you have learned in reaching maturity at the gaming tables, will more than assist you in any business or profession you might want to become a part of. This I have MANY TIMES seen to be a proven fact.

As for the casino or the casino personnel, don't for one second worry about their having to declare either personal or corporate bankruptcy, becasue of what I have just written. I'll lay a price of 20 to 1 that they won't lose ½ of 1% of their customers. (Unless the customers continue betting their money as they do now, and go broke.) You may believe me when I say, if I live another 30 lifetimes, that I'VE SEEN ENOUGH LOSERS. I'd like to see a few more winners for a change. In my role as The Dice Doctor, *I'M SURE I CAN BE OF SOME HELP.*

Would you believe that many longtime crapshooters are actually embarrassed to play at a CASINO CRAP TABLE?? The numerous printed bets on the crap table layout are new to them. These crapshooters have played army craps, alley craps, stag craps, fade craps and in all probability, at floating crap games, where all they used was a deck of cards to show the Pass Line Point and the box numbers etc.

Many of these potential customers are understandably hesitant when they see the CHRISTMAS TREE LAYOUT on a casino crap table. The casino and casino personnel could do much more in helping the new casino crapshooter understand the different bets. Granted, they will give you a Gaming Guide, (if you ask for one) or the odd casino does have an instructor give an outline on gaming either on in-house TV or in person at the tables.

What every crapshooter should know, is that any form of craps can be played on a casino crap table. The only difference would be whether or not you pay the House the juice (commission), that you DON'T PAY when you play at army craps, stag craps, fade craps etc., but that you DO PAY at casino or any other type of BANK CRAPS. (Floating crap games or run and cut games.)

I have many times heard these non-casino crapshooters as spectators, complain that they would feel embarrassed in front of their women or friends if they made a couple of boo boos. (Because of the difference of THEIR play and that of the CASINO PLAY.) To me, it would be heart-breaking, if as a pointholder or as a shareholder, I were to see these POTENTIAL customers walk PAST my crap table, instead of UP TO my crap table. Just because my employees didn't give a damn whether they played or not.

Isn't it sickening to watch certain of the pit personnel catering and glad-handing the weak or stupid player?? And then turn around and glare at a more knowledgeable player or dealer that wants to help. This is a fallacy on the part of the House, as has been proven by the tremendous increase in the game of 21 (or blackjack) in the past 25 years. This increase has been brought about by salesmanship. Because of reasonably priced books, that show how, for a few dollars, any player could learn a decent BASIC STRATEGY and have an almost EVEN UP SHOT versus the House. In the meantime, DUE TO THE WEAKNESS OF HUMAN NATURE, the House STILL wound up with a fair share of the player's buck.

As for the Advanced Strategy in blackjack?? Good luck to those mathematical geniuses who can handle it. (WITHOUT GETTING BARRED OR SHUFFLED UP ON FOR CARD COUNTING.) I'm glad there's no such thing as "advanced strategy" in the crap game. Enough crapshooters have trouble figuring out the correct payoff on a $12 Place Bet on the 6 or 8.

30, 40 or more years ago, most good crapshooters were also good CARD CASERS, or as they now like to be called, CARD COUNTERS. This was a bit of an edge that we had going for ourselves. At that time, most of the joints dealt SINGLE DECK, which wasn't then, nor is it now, such a big deal to case. (Or to count.) The one big difference between ourselves and many of the new Blackjack Touts or self-styled experts, we knew enough to KEEP OUR MOUTH SHUT and not brag about our ability to COUNT CARDS.

I don't recall even ONE card caser being barred. Occasionally the odd pit boss would ask us to be nice and come back on another pit boss' shift. So much for 21 or blackjack. Let's get back to the crap game.

I'm sure that all casino and floating crap game operators like their chances. As business people, they should accept that a larger turnover at the tables, including even that small percentage of MATURE players, will not be the cause of them or their employees standing on street corners with tin cups.

The system players, the weak players, the longshot or idiot players, will more than make up for the small minority who are mature players. This has been the case in my more than 50 years as a bettor and as a bookie. I doubt that the next 50 years will be much different. (I hope I'm wrong. I'VE SEEN ENOUGH LOSERS!)

The successful gambler accepts that he will have losing streaks. His training has prepared him for ONE OR MANY CONSECUTIVE LOSSES. A good money manager will NOT double up in an effort to regain his losses. The opposite is closer to the truth in that he would be more apt to REDUCE the size of his betting stakes. He knows from experience, that DIMES WILL BECOME DOLLARS, if and when the dice turn for him. ONE GOOD ONE MAKES UP FOR MANY BAD ONES, is a cliche' quote the smart money manager is entitled to use.

The PROFESSIONAL in contrast to 99% of the players, accepts the fact when you lose your first $100 or your first $1000, that it is NO LONGER YOUR MONEY. Your original bankroll is now EXACTLY THE REMAINING BALANCE!

Being human, we find it difficult to accept this reality. However, even a small step in this direction, will give you a more mature outlook towards gambling.

It could help you overcome sleepless nights, sexless nights, frustrations, impotence, anger outbursts plus many other bad traits of the average gambler.

You may stop blaming the dealer, the dice, the man next to you at the crap table, or even an excited wife who rushes up to you at the crap table to show you the $10 she won at the nickel slot machine!! You in turn (if you don't accept this loss fact) could be blowing your brains out, BY DOUBLING UP AND MAKING EVERY SUCKER BET

ON THE TABLE, just trying to win back your losses. (Usually it's a few dollars more than your wife's $10 win at the slots.)

Trying to overcome this human fault, won't guarantee you more winning bets, but it might help towards your reaching that ELUSIVE MATURITY at the gaming tables. In other words, don't try forcing the game. Just hope you are lucky enough to be at a crap table if or when a hand or shoot shows. My set of betting rules will show you EXACTLY what to do.

Being at the RIGHT TABLE at the RIGHT TIME, is just another cliche' quote. This is DUMB LUCK. But winning $200 or $2000 on the SAME HAND with the SAME initial bet, is not luck. IT IS SENSIBLE PROGRESSIVE BETTING!!

Don't be envious of the player who is raking in winning bets from all over the craps layout. ANY bet you care to make at the crap table can be won. Not once, but AGAIN and AGAIN. This does not mean you are making smart bets. Just the opposite. THIS AGAIN IS DUMB LUCK! Sooner or later, (usually sooner) YOU WILL HIT THE BRICK WALL!! I'm a real authority on hitting brick walls. I went that route for many expensive years, before reaching what I like to call MY MATURITY AT THE CRAP TABLES.

Let's spend a few minutes talking about the dealers. Considering their ability and responsibilities, dealers wages without the tips are very low. A common saying by the dealer, is that a SMALL GEORGE (small tipper) is better than NO GEORGE. Whereas a REAL or SUPER GEORGE (big or biggest tipper) helps the dealer forget that he is just plain working for peanuts. (Sorry, ex-pres Carter. It was just a PLAIN slip of the tongue.)

Dealers who are sincere and aggressive, do in time move up the ladder where their wages improve. As a matter of fact, I don't know of any business or profession that even begins to compare with the gaming business. In what other profession, can you go to school for 6 to 12 weeks, spend between $250 and $1000 in tuition fees, and then go to work for 15 to 25 thousand a year, TO START WITH??

In Las Vegas, tips are usually split up table for table. In Atlantic City tips are divided among ALL dealers. (Regardless as to which game they deal, or what shift they work.) Craps dealers prefer table for table. It's sickening to dealers that have to carry the load for the deadbeat, and then give him an equal share of the tokes. In Vegas, they really work and hustle for their tokes. In Atlantic City, they are just now learning how to say THANK YOU when a player makes a bet for them, or throws them a tip. (Oh well. Give them time and short-roll toke boxes. THEY'LL LEARN!)

Dealers pray for the big or monster hand to show at THEIR table. They stand a good chance of winding up with some serious money in tips.

A dealer who isn't under too much HEAT from the pit personnel or boxman, can help a weak player in many ways. You may occasionally run into a MISFIT. They don't (unless they're loaded with JUICE) last too long. The other three members of the crew, NEED HIM LIKE A HOLE IN THE HEAD, both personally and financially. In other words, don't cover all dealers with the SAME BLANKET. Close to 100% of all casino personnel were BREAK-IN DEALERS at the start of their careers. (From Casino boss on down. Some of them seem to forget it!!)

One of the first rules (requirements, prerequisites or whatever) of joining the gaming profession, is that YOU MUST BE ABLE TO HANDLE THE GAMBLING SCENE!! This is an unfortunate short or long-term problem with far too many casino people, from the bottom (the break-in dealer) to the top. (Casino boss.) I've seen them both.

With the gaming industry expanding towards a multi-billion dollar LEGITIMATE business, (it has for many years been a multi-billion dollar ILLEGITIMATE business) I feel it is more than about time that they had an organization formed, to help keep casino employees from becoming candidates for Gamblers anonymous. (I believe that something has been started in New Jersey as I was writing this.) I most certainly hope so. I've seen many capable casino people go down the drain, when just a bit of honest advice might have prevented it from happening to many of them. Of course, in a large number of cases, you could have stood on your head in front of the City Hall, and preached to them all day. It wouldn't have helped. (Or as they say in Italian, ES VET GORNISHT HELFEN!!)

If potentially sick gamblers could hear some of the heart-breaking therapy at a Gamblers Anonymous meeting, they might stand a chance of preventing this from happening to themselves. The best advice I can give to you guys and gals that are considering becoming a part of the gaming industry, is to LEAVE THE GAMBLING TO TOURISTS!!

SERVICE and COURTESY are and always has been, mainly what the Gaming Industry had to offer. This was the case with the horse books, the floating crap games, the sports books, as well as the legal and illegal casinos. With the exception of where you had THE ONLY GAME IN TOWN, you knew that you had to show a bit of class, if you wanted a customer to partronize YOUR JOINT rather than one of a dozen OTHER JOINTS.

Nothing has changed in either the legal or illegal gaming industry. It has only EXPANDED. Make top service, courtesy and a sincere personality your goal, and you can expect the results to be personally and financially very rewarding. Although to a certain extent, the "juice" or pull is still A FACT OF LIFE, (inside AND outside the gaming industry) just prove you are capable and willing, and I'll lay a price on your making it WITHOUT THE JUICE.

There are a couple of other bits of advice, I would like to give to the break-in dealer, the new boxman or the new floor person. (Or any other "1500 hour wonder".) Don't hop, skip and jump from one job to another. Because of temporary conditions in Atlantic City, you may find it quite easy to find another job. However, I can almost give you a written guarantee, that you won't become a member of any permanent team. (Or a dependable loyal employee.) This advice is as good, outside the gaming industry.

As a break-in dealer, listen to your boxman. He may at times antagonize you or BUST YOUR ASS, but he more than anyone else, can help make a good dealer out of you, and start you on your way up the ladder.

Talking about break-in dealers. In September of 1978 when I first went to Atlantic City after legalized gambling took hold, (I was last there in 1936) I would gladly have recommended 40% or 50% of the dealers for an audition at ANY Strip Hotel in Las Vegas. The jam-up action at the crap tables, had in just a few months "dealing live", easily compared to at least two years dealing in Las Vegas. Courtesy and personality-wise, I'm sorry to say, I wouldn't have recommended nearly so many. It's unfortunate that when they took their 12 weeks dealers' course, that the teachers didn't take a couple of hours and teach them how to deal with the players, as well as with the players' chips.

I certainly never thought I would live to see the "jam-up" action that's today taking place in Atlantic City. Las Vegas took more than 50 years to reach today's earning level. Give Atlantic City 50 months, and I'll lay a price that dollar-wise she'll TOP Las Vegas.

I'm not taking too much of a chance in making this bet. Atlantic City is within comfortable driving distance of 50 million people. Of these 50 million, 49½ million are gamblers. (Albeit they are the world's worst gamblers, and the most stubborn to boot.)

In their wildest dreams, Atlantic City casino owners never dreamed that these Easterners would (by the way they don't give their money a chance) almost beg the casinos to take their money. I've seen quite a number of Easterners on Junkets to Las Vegas, and I've even respected the play of many of them. But here on their home grounds, YOU WOULD HAVE TO SWEAR THAT THEY WERE PLAYING WITH QUEER (counterfeit) MONEY. (Which according to the papers, some of them were.)

I agree that I'm sarcastic at times. However, if taking a bit of sarcasm will help the weak player, then please accept that it's a very small price to pay. (I paid MUCH more.) I play or teach the game of craps, practically every day. I DO see players literally DESTROYING THEMSELVES by their overall bad play.

In Las Vegas, the majority of players appreciate it when a dealer or a more knowledgeable player points out an error in his moves. Here in the East however, not only don't they graciously accept your helpful suggestions, (be it a dealer, a pit person, or a knowledgeable player at the same table) but to add insult to their ignorance, they won't even say thank you when they DO admit they are wrong.

There's an old cliche' saying: Gambling SOMETIMES brings out the worst in people. Don't you believe it!! Gambling will ALWAYS bring out the worst.

Please excuse my wandering from time to time. I'm a practicing crapshooter, not an author. Also, since the crap game interfered with my academic education, don't expect a Pulitzer prize winning novel. The awards that my students and I are looking for, can ONLY be found at the CASHIER'S CAGE.

O.K. Let's get back to what we came here for in the first place. The casino crap game.

My set of BASIC STRATEGY BETTING RULES deals only with the Pass Line, plus the taking of SINGLE or DOUBLE ODDS. (Depending on your personal bankroll, and the casino you are playing in.)

Following are all the moves necessary in my Method of Play. The PROGRESSIVE BETTING CHART, which also includes the BETTING STAKE CHART, is the ONLY CHART we will need. Contrary to what most system peddlers would have you believe, properly played, craps is VERY EASY to learn. Improperly played, these same CRAP TABLE TOUTS, would have you believe that you need a college degree in computer mathematics. One other point of value. Modern crap tables, unlike the older type, (they had a SINGLE groove for holding your chips) have DOUBLE GROOVES, making it much easier to MANAGE YOUR MONEY. (Floating crap games, usually use pool tables or covered ¾" sheets of plywood.)

I do not like to call my Method of Play a system as such. The reason being, that in every known system "the chasing of your money" is customary. I have eliminated 95% of all the chasing, and even this 5% is more than overcome by the SMARTEST BET on the Crap Table. (When I use the words "smartest bet" in a Minus Factor or House Edge game, please believe that I am merely comparing it to other more expensive House Edge bets.) I won't insult your intelligence by guaranteeing any bet on the Crap Table. (Except one.)

MONEY MANAGEMENT . . . PATIENCE. . . SENSIBLE PROGRESSIVE BETTING.
. . (Sensible expansion in the "business world") are rules which may be used in all
forms of gambling, as well as in any business or profession. Small adjustments are all
that are usually necessary.

The end goal is the same. In gambling you must always LIMIT YOUR LOSSES . . .
NEVER LIMIT YOUR WINNINGS. In the business world, TRY TO LIMIT YOUR
MISTAKES . . . NEVER LIMIT YOUR ACCOMPLISHMENTS. In gambling, you can
definitely limit your losses to the LAST DOLLAR. In the business and professional
world, you can ony "try" to LIMIT YOUR MISTAKES.

One thing is certain, my Method of Play and Set of Betting Rules (although they
carry no guarantee) will not hurt ONE person who is ANYWAYS intent on gambling. I
will qualify this statment by saying, IF YOU PERSONALLY ARE A CANDIDATE FOR
GAMBLERS ANONYMOUS, then you are not included. Even a written guarantee that
you will win, won't help. Unfortunately, you are (if lucky) a temporarily SICK person.
Forget gambling and put your efforts to work in ANY other direction. Sick or
compulsive gamblers are usually very shrewd and capable. (How else do you think
they work their con plays on their friends or families to get that next betting stake??)

Once you get your head screwed on straight, I'LL BOOK EVEN MONEY that you
will make it as far and as fast as you care to. I'm not kidding or throwing out any
bouquets when I say this. Having been around gambling all my life, it stands to
reason that I've run into my share of "sickies".

I've seen more than enough heartaches, heartbreaks and misery. At the same time,
I can say that I've been lucky enough to see quite a few of these sick people straighten
out. Fortunately, in my business and environment, I don't see them after they go
clean. The Casino, the race track or the floating crap game is the last place that we
would care to see each other. (I much prefer being a guest at their six month or ten
year STAYING CLEAN pinning at a Gamblers Anonymous meeting.)

I'm not a missionary or a do-gooder. I make a nice quiet living at the Crap Table. At
the same time, and although I DON'T advocate gambling, I DO try to help those who
CAN handle the crap table without hurting themselves and others. (I wouldn't give a
sick or compulsive gambler the price of a 25¢ ticket at a church raffle.)

I have always had a soft spot for the weak gambler, even when I was a part or full
owner of a crap game. I never made money my God. I never owned a Cadillac. There
were times in the thirties when a night's winnings could have bought me a Rolls
Royce. To me, the crap game is, and always has been a highly over-rated challenge. I
never did, and I still don't accept that in the long run, the House will grind you out.
Granted that they have an edge, but if any crapshooter can show a winning batting
average over a period of time lasting many years, then don't tell me that it's a written
guarantee that you MUST lost your money. Show me a good money manager with a
sensible Method of Play, and I'll gladly back a piece of his action with my own money.
The one thing that I regret most about being a gambler, is that accomplishment-wise
and family-wise, THE GREATEST GAMBLER IN THE WORLD HAS LESS THAN
NOTHING TO BRAG ABOUT.

Can you picture your children telling their friends that their father is the greatest
gambler in the world?? Can you picture your wife telling her friends that her husband
is a successful gambler?? Being a top mechanic, or a good short order cook, would
carry MUCH MORE prestige. THINK ABOUT IT!! You may want to return this book

for a refund. Or better yet, keep it as a worthwhile reminder.

Please bare with me if my writing is not up to your literary standards. I'm a Teacher of Craps, a Doctor of Dice and a practicing Crapshooter. NOT AN AUTHOR!! I spent more time, more money, more sleepless nights and more mental anguish, in serving my apprenticeship and paying my tuition fees, than many an author, doctor, academic professional or businessman. In plain English children, I PAID MY DUES!!

At that I consider myself very fortunate. I've known many other gamblers who spent the same 50 years, and as much or more money and they still haven't reached maturity at the gaming tables. I feel that I have. Otherwise it would be presumptuous of me to tell another man (or woman) how to gamble THEIR money.

Getting back to the Betting Stake and the Lock-up Rack. Should you at any time wish to leave the table while your Betting Stake is in action (play), count and write down separately, the amounts in your Betting Stake (or front) Groove and in your Lock-up (or rear) Groove. When ready to resume play, return to the same table and replace the chips (or checks) in their proper grooves. (Providing of course that the same table is open and in action. Otherwise you would move on to the next table consecutively numbered that IS open, replacing the same number of checks at THAT table.)

Should you go to another Casino for a show or a dinner, and decide to play in that Casino, then just continue as though you were at the original casino where you had interrupted your play. The only thing you would do different would be to go to Table #1 or #2 etc. and continue your play, as though you hadn't left the other hotel.

Play can be resumed an hour later, a month later, or the day after your three year-old daughter gets married. As far as the dice are concerned, a washroom break, a show or a shower break, or a trip to the South Sea Islands are the same thing. The dice have trouble remembering what they did on their last roll, so there's little chance of them knowing what they'll do on their next roll. As for the dice "having eyes", don't believe it. I've had them examined by my brother-in-law Phil, a well qualified optometrist. He agrees that the dice are BLIND. P.S. Phil, send an itemized bill to the publisher. He'll send you a check by return mail.

My goal in writing a book on Craps, is to make the casual as well as the regular Crapshooter stop and think how to give his GAMBLING MONEY a GAMBLING CHANCE. This includes making all decisions as to EXACTLY how you are going to bet BEFORE you walk up to the Crap Table. Everything we do in our lives is planned out in advance, EXCEPT when we go to gamble. (Even the horse players that spend hours handicapping a card, will completely ignore their selections when they get into the line to buy their tickets.)

Another immature remark often heard from the Crapshooter, is that he is going to see what the dice are doing and then bet Right or Wrong accordingly. He won't accept the fact that it only takes ONE TURN of the dice to change a HOT table to ICE and vice versa. Do yourself and your gambling money a favor. Make all your decisions BEFORE you make your first bet.

It's unfortunate that many players are so fascinated with the XMAS TREE LAYOUT containing all those expensive proposition bets. I realize that without those gravy bets (for the House) that many of these crap games would be operated in road-side motels, instead of multi-million dollar hotels. It would however, be a nice gesture on the part of the casinos if they would place little signs around those proposition bets saying, THESE ARE SUCKER BETS . . . PLAY AT YOUR OWN RISK!! Don't laugh!

Most crapshooters would STILL bet on them.

As a Doctor of Dice (Teacher) I've been called on to help with some pretty weak plays. One player in particular had a hang-up on HORN BETS. (1-1, 1-2, 6-6, 6-5)

Regardless of any other bets he might make, he always had a Horn Bet going. I told him that the expensive House Edge made it a very weak bet. He agreed, but said it was only a small portion of his overall dollar betting, and that the kicks he got out of hitting these Horn Bets, made it worth the extra P.C. he had to come up with.

He recalled once running into eight consecutive Horn numbers, and didn't know how to handle them. He was wealthy enough (at the time) to cater to his whims, so I came up with the following play. (You're right!! It WAS embarrassing.) The dealers and the pit personnel whom I knew personally, wouldn't let me live it down.

We wait for the shooter to roll the first Horn number. (In keeping with the truism that a shooter must roll the first of any number, before he can possibly roll the second or third or whatever of the SAME number. (Or as in our case, the Horn numbers.) We now make our first bet of four (4) units. One unit on each of the four Horn numbers. Should the shooter roll a second consecutive Horn number, we would then double th size of our bets on each of the Horn numbers. We continue doubling our bets as long as consecutive Horn numbers are rolled.

I haven't seen this player in some time, but I'm willing to lay a price, that his bankroll is somewhat lighter.

My only consolation in helping this player with his IDIOT PLAY, is that I taught him HOW TO PLAY LIKE AN INTELLIGENT IDIOT.

I know I've said it before, and I'll probably repeat it. I DON'T ADVOCATE GAMBLING. But if you must gamble, then try the crap tables.

There are apparently certain types of illness, (possibly mental depression?) that reacts more favorably to the adrenalin flow at the crap table, then the benefits one might receive form other forms of treatment. (Be it group therapy or placebo, IT WORKS!!)

I am NOT trained in medicine. I have however by PEOPLE WATCHING, both as an employee and as a player (at the crap games), seen what I felt were THERAPEUTIC benefits that certain people get at the crap table, or just in the casino itself. (As I said, I'm not trained in medicine and I could be spouting off without knowing my A from a H in the ground. If so, my apologies to the medical profession for talking out of line.)

Also, I was certainly NOT referring to Gamblers Anonymous candidates. THEY unfortunately, are headed for the bottom with or without any help. Unless these candidates honestly admit they are compulsive gamblers, and for their own as well as their family's sake, want to give up gambling entirely, you can expect a whole new wave of these hapless unfortunates.

If you think I'm kidding, then just listen to this. Atlantic City (at the time of writing) has been (legitimately) in action, just over 7 years. The South Philly "smart money action boys" have already gone through their bankrolls 3 or 4 times at the casino tables, 20% of the area businessmen are hurting from personal casino losses.

Do you honestly think for one minute, that ordinary everyday Gamblers Anonymous candidates stand a chance in ANY state with legalized gambling?? As for financial returns a state can EXPECT, compared to the personal losses it can GUARANTEE?? YOU GOTTA BE KIDDING!!

Nevada could fill the bill as an exception. (Almost) It takes 5 hours by car to get there from an INHABITED STATE.

I shouldn't refer to Nevada so sarcastically. (I really love that state.) It does have one of the healthiest climates in the U.S. (When they are not testing the bomb.) You can indulge in most sports year round.

It's just too bad that the corporations together with their computers, (they have that one-track BOTTOM LINE mind) took over from the "BOYS". The last 15 or 18 years in Las Vegas, haven't been the same.

At least when the KIDS were in charge, you could day or night, go anywhere. The BOYS made it loud and clear that anybody who mugged a tourist OR a local, was stealing from them. (THE BOYS.)

Vegas has always had more than enough crime, but not as much as there is today. With utmost respect for our local police, who of necessity must be every bit as good or better than any in the country, I don't recommend your going a block off the main streets after sundown. (Unfortunately, this advice holds good for MOST of the bigger cities throughout the country.)

Las Vegas being an OPEN CITY, even the BOYS themselves live a more PEACEFUL life than elsewhere. (Except blah, blah, in Florida.) When THEY put on a charitable affair, it is a guaranteed success whose sale of tickets YOU JUST CAN'T REFUSE!! (Gee, do we really get to rub elbows with such notoriety?) Bullshaloney!! You couldn't recognize them as being any different than you and I, even if we slept in the same oversize bed together. Personally, I for one don't want to know, or care to see, what goes on in their bedrooms or behind closed doors. If they can teach me something new about the crap game, then I'll listen and say, THANK YOU SIR!! In other words children, forget it. Don't learn the hard way. There are enough GREEN SPOTS in the desert.

As I've mentioned before, it takes a five hour drive from civilization to get to the Las Vegas DRY CLEANING PLANTS. (The casinos.) Drive five hours from Atlantic City or any of the other future casino cities in the East, and you are reaching between 50 and 60 million CASINO VIRGINS. God help these ALLEY CRAPS AMATEURS if they don't take a little time and effort to prepare themselves, and possibly prevent a SLAUGHTER.

COME BETS?? THEY AIN'T NO BARGAIN!!

Proposition bets, such as C&E (craps or eleven), horn bets, Big Red (7), Big 6 or 8, hard ways, field bets, place bets, and even the misunderstood COME BETS, these (with the exception of the Come Bets that I call "semi-bad" bets) are ALL weak bets because of the more expensive House Edge you must give up. These are the bets that go a long way towards building those palace-like hotels.

I would like to qualify my reasons for calling the COME BET a SEMI-BAD BET. Certain self-styled experts may disagree with my reasoning. Practically every article you may read on Come Bets, claim them to be the same as the Pass Line Bet, after a Pass Line Point has been established.

My reason for disputing this claim is as follows: The shooter has established a point on the Pass Line. He now makes a Come Bet. He may continue making as many Come Bets as he wishes. Or until he sevens out.

Let us assume that the player has one or more Come Bets on the Layout, and then makes his Pass Line Point. When the player made his initial bet on the Pass Line, he hoped that he could start by rolling a Natural (7 or 11), or better yet, a lot of Naturals. Now that he has made his Pass Line Point, and since he has one or as many as six (6) Come Bets in action, he would welcome an eleven (11) on the Come-out Roll for a new Pass Line Point. However, the VERY LAST number he now wants to see is the seven (7).

With a seven on the Come-out Roll for a new point, he would of course win the FLAT PORTION of his Pass Line Bet. The ODDS PORTION of his Come Bet (or bets)would be returned to him. (Unless he had his odds WORKING on the Come-out Roll. Which is a STUPID MOVE.) The House would win the FLAT PORTION of his Come Bets. In a SINGLE ODDS game, the flat portion could be approximately half of his entire bet. In a DOUBLE ODDS game, the flat portion would be a third of his entire bet. In TRIPLE, QUINTUPLE or TEN TIMES ODDS, correspondingly less.

This should confirm my argument with fellow DICE AUTHORITIES?? That Come Bets, although while in action, are identical to the Pass Line Bet, they are NOT by the furthest stretch of the imagination, the same as the COMPLETE pass-line bet!! To win ONE part bet, or to lose ONE OR AS MANY AS SIX part bets, on one roll of the dice, IS NOT THE SAME.

One COMPUTER CRAPSHOOTER, (No dice. . . No chips . . . No crap table. . . No nothing) claims that my reasoning is comparable to a blind Russian, playing Chinese checkers in the middle of the Rio Grande River, between El Paso, Texas and Juarez, Mexico. (Come again??) He also claims, "quote". If the Pass Line were eliminated from the Craps Layout, that the Come Line would take its place . . . To which I answer, "quote". If my grandmother had been blessed with a pair of nuts, then she could possibly have been my grandfather. (His quote makes as little or less sense than mine.)

In other words, my dear COMPUTER CRAPSHOOTER, if you are a beginner (or a neophyte) as you claim, then leave the crap table layout as is, and stick to your TOYS and your MASS NUMBERS. Leave the crap table to the crapshooter who has learned to count from 1 to 10.

In a following article I will show you how to CONVERT the Come Bets, in a way that will help to overcome some of the weaker features of the NORMAL Come Betting.

As for the choice of Come Betting versus Place or Buy Betting, many players (correctly) insist that Place and Buy Betting gave you a win when your number showed for the FIRST TIME. Whereas in Come Betting, your number must show TWICE for you to win a bet. What the Place or Buy bettor seems to forget, is that your Come Bet number DID at least show for that first time, whereas any Place or Buy number or numbers YOU select, may not show at ANY TIME you are on them.

Want my advice? Let the rolls of the dice do the HANDICAPPING and tell you which number (or numbers) to bet on. THEY ARE NOT GUESSING!! When you pick certain numbers, you are guessing!!

PAST PERFORMANCES

Past performances may occasionally help you in handicapping a horse race or a sporting event. Past performances however, are less than useless at a Crap Table, a Baccarat table, or a Roulette table. Past performances at the Blackjack table, could be of some use to the Card Counter.

The ability to count cards does not give you a guarantee that you will win. Although serious money has at times been won by card counters, (so claims so and so, in the book he had published) card counters have also run into long periods of losses, and in many cases have lost their entire bankrolls. (So said the same writer.)

P.S. I didn't have to read this. I was approached by the head of a card-counting team, to lend him $2000 to get him and his team back to Las Vegas from Atlantic City. This happened when the Atlantic City Casinos opened to the card counters for 12 or 13 days in 1979. They were to have given the counters 30 days, but because of real or imagined losses, they barred them again after those 12 or 13 days. Card counters can no longer be barred in New Jersey.

If members of this particular card counting team are reading this, I'm still waiting for the $1000 that you finally mooched me out of. I'll settle for 30¢ on the dollar!!

To certain PARANOID WRITERS on blackjack who insist the dealers are DEALING SECONDS or STACKING DECKS in the CASINO'S favor, all I can say, is that you are a bunch of poor losers. You were beat fair and square. Your gambling money in many cases was put up by OTHERS than yourselves, (BACKERS) and you wanted to blame someone else for either your bad luck or your BAD PLAY. (I don't work for the casinos, so don't get the idea that I'm being paid for saying these things. I DO get "comped" to a bowl of corn flakes once in awhile.)

You'll get a SQUARE GAME in 99.9% of ALL legitimate casinos. I'll even go further and say that MOST operators of FLOATING GAMES are HONORABLE PEOPLE. However, there's always a chance that you could wind up in a BUSTOUT JOINT. Just know the people who refer you to these floating games. Should you run into one of these games, don't complain that it was "THE ONLY GAME IN TOWN".

The fact that the counter may at times have a Big Percentage (plus factor) Edge against the dealer, it is still quite possible for the dealer or one of the non card counting players to get the good hands that the counter had hoped would be dealt to him. Also, the Plus Factor in Blackjack, if at all, could only be of use in the dealing of the CURRENT deck or shoe, and not in any FUTURE decks or shoes.

You can see then, that past performances at their best, CARRIES NO GUARANTEE. A good example of the value of past performances , dollar-wise, is that for $2.95 each you can buy the following books . . . ROULETTE (25,000 decisions) . . . Baccarat (25,000 random hands) or 72 HOURS at the CRAP TABLE. Although these are a terrific value for working out systems that use sunflower seeds for betting stakes, ALL COMBINED, THEY COULD NOT GUARANTEE YOU ONE WINNING BET.

DICE TRENDS

I won't spend or WASTE too much time on this subject. It is of NO value at the CRAP TABLE. Some writers on dice have come up with a supposedly new method of handicapping the future rolls of the dice.

All dealers, as well as many everyday CRAPSHOOTERS, occasionally get the feeling they are seeing a group of consecutive IDENTICAL NUMBERS that they had seen before. NO! You are NOT PSYCHIC!! What IS happening, is that after many rolls of the dice, series of numbers must eventually repeat themselves. More so and more often when you only have 36 combinations on a pair of dice to work with.

Were you to go through sheets containing many random rolls of the dice, I am sure that you could quite easily pick out shorter or longer series of numbers in identical sequence. (These are the times when the ESP specialists believe they have something going for them.)

Again I'll repeat. Past Performances or Dice Trends at the Crap Table are JUST THAT. They are of NO VALUE at the PRESENT or in the FUTURE. At best, they could be conversation pieces, after they've taken place.

To those potential authors who think they can come up with something where the past performances or the dice trends can help the crapshooter, all I can say, and in all sincerity, is to FORGET IT!!

DUE BETS

From time to time, many gamblers will bet on what they believe to be a DUE BET. They fool themselves into thinking that mathematically, a winning hand or shoot is DUE at the Crap Table. That a red or black, an odd or even, etc. is DUE at the Roulette Table. A banker or player hand is DUE at the Baccarat Table. All or any of these DUE BETS, the same as PAST PERFORMANCES, mean absolutely nothing. In HONEST gambling, there is no such thing as a GUARANTEED winning bet, taking place on the next turn of the cards, or roll of the dice.

You will often see players with a pad and pencil, writing down numbers at the Roulette or Baccarat tables. Do these CENSUS TAKERS a favor and tell them about the books they can buy for $2.95 that contain the 25,000 random hands at the Baccarat Table, or the 25,000 random rolls on the Roulette Table. As for the person at the Crap Table with a pad and pencil--he could be doing one of two things. (A) Trying to handicap the rolls of the dice--which is a waste of time. (B) He is a Crap Table HUSTLER, waiting for a LIVE MARK to inquire about his system, and perhaps falling into the HUSTLER'S TRAP.

DEBUNKING SYSTEMS

Any and all systems DO WORK. (At times.) I have as yet to run into a system that won't work. It's only that some systems have a higher fatality rate than others. Eventually they all die. Unfortunately the system player has no way of knowing whether it will work for hours, for days, or even longer. Or whether HE WILL HIT THE BRICK WALL and go broke on the first shooter or shooters.

I won't say that all gamblers haven't time and again dreamed of someday coming up with a winning system. But let's not insult our own intelligence by honestly believing that it can ever happen . . . legitimately. No matter how small, when there is a MINUS FACTOR in the gamble, then the only chance you have is to use the three basics of successful gambling. MONEY MANAGEMENT . . . PATIENCE . . .SENSIBLE PROGRESSIVE BETTING.

The same systems keep popping up every few years under different names!! The crap table tout, who can be compared to the race track tout, never seems to run short of SUCKER LISTS to sell these systems to.

Granted, all betting should follow a systematic rather than a random approach. However, the difference between playing the outright CHASING SYSTEMS, such as 1-2-4-8-etc., where the successful result is a SINGLE minimum unit or so. Whereas in our method of plays, a winning result could be anywheres from a single unit, to as much as the TABLE LIMIT on another winning decision. Putting it in crap table lingo: in the normal playing of systems, the player could be chasing a PEANUT with a PALM

TREE . . . or your entire betting stake against the smallest possible net win. In my METHODS of PLAY, it could be the reverse, in that the House could be chasing YOUR PEANUT (or minimum bet) with THEIR PALM TREE, or ENTIRE CASINO BANKROLL.

Even the most sophisticated systems, uselessly put together by mathematicians, can quite easily be broken down to where the average nine-year-old can understand and play them. I'm not intentially knocking the capable mathematician. What I am asking them to do, is to stick to their academics that sent man to the moon, and may someday help us find a cure for Multiple Sclerosis or Muscular Dystrophy, or even Cancer. Let those of us that just learned to count form 1 to 10 plus STREETS EDUCATION, handle the crap game.

Since I've personally helped players improve on systems they INSISTED on playing, I must assume a certain amount of guilt. Still, I do at all times make it loud and clear that I don't approve of ANY plays that call for the chasing and increasing of the size of losing bets. This covers every known system including IDIOT PLAYS that as The Dice Doctor, I am also called on to help with. The most I have been able to do for these weak players, is TEACH THEM TO PLAY LIKE AN INTELLIGENT IDIOT!!

THE SUCCESSFUL GAMBLER MUST GRIND

Contrary to what you may hear or believe, the successful gambler MUST GRIND! There is no such thing as his TAKING SHOTS. He depends on his SENSIBLE PROGRESSIVE BETTING when a hand or a shoot shows. The profit hands, small--big--or MONSTER, will show in their own sweet time. The player who PLAYS FOR KEEPS will get his share. In the meantime, due to his PATIENCE and ability to MANAGE HIS MONEY, he will hold his losses to a minimum.

Unlike the majority of players, the successful gambler has NO PITY on the House. It is hard to believe the number of players who are almost APOLOGETIC to the House, when they make a win!! On the other hand, they ACTUALLY BRAG about their losses!! Personally, I don't want either their pity OR their congratulations. I JUST WANT THEIR MONEY. (Plus all the "comps" I can get for giving my action to THEM, rather than to another joint.)

The House works on actuary principles.* (*Throw enough shit on the wall, and some is bound to stick . . . or to be more genteel. Give us the turnover, WE'LL GET OURS.)

The House DOES get hurt from time to time. The best break a casino can hope for when the big or MONSTER hand shows, is for the hi-rollers and tough players to be in the toilet WITH A BAD CASE OF DIARRHEA. The less than 1% House Edge that the tough players give up, doesn't go too far towards building their palace-like hotels. (They might help pay for the ash trays and the toilet paper.)

The successful player is not surprised when he wins. He feels he DESERVED to win because of the time and effort he put into preparing himself to win. When he loses, the House knows that THEY won it THE HARD WAY!

The mature player is usually a pleasure for the dealing crew and the pit personnel to have at their table. He is quiet. Doesn't hassle the dealers. He is courteous to the other players at the table, and can afford the luxury of TRYING to be helpful to the weaker or less knowledgeable players. (I did say TRY to be helpful.)

Some of these players are not only weak, but rude, stubborn and arrogant as well. Should you run into these mistakes of human nature, just ignore them. Let them learn the hard way . . . THROUGH THE POCKET!!

For mercenary as well as personal reasons, dealers DO try to help the player. They have learned from day one that COURTESY and SERVICE will go a long way towards filling their TOKE BOXES. (This is how it was in 1929 when I broke in as a dealer.) Not too much has changed.

GETTING OVER THE HUMP

Probably the most useless words in any form of gambling, is GETTING OVER THE HUMP. I've made that remark many times myself, before reaching the conclusion that there just AIN'T NO SUCH THING.

Here are just a couple of examples that I've run into. They may help you reach the same decision. Your accepting that this is just another fallacy, could be a big step towards your reaching maturity at the Crap Table, or any other form of gambling. (Or business venture.)

I was watching the play on a crap table at the ALADDIN HOTEL CASINO in Las Vegas. A gambling junket had just arrived from Detroit. One of the junketeers came to the table and signed a MARKER (casino check) for $2000 in chips. The previous shooter had just sevened out, and the stickman pushed the dice to the next shooter. The junketeer proceeded to BET THE LAYOUT. He took Double Odds behind his Pass-line Bet. He Placed and Bought the other 5 numbers. He bet all the hardways, and then made a $200 Come Bet. As luck would have it, the shooter started rolling what would wind up to be A MONSTER OF A HAND.

To make a long story short, when the shooter finally sevened out, the junketeer had the Table Limit on all the numbers and hardways, plus a few limit Come Bets. He won more than $55,000 on this ONE hand. What do you think was his gem of a remark?? JUST A FEW MORE NUMBERS AND I WOULD HAVE BEEN OVER THE HUMP!!

This DETROIT DESTROYER (whom I've seen in several repeat performances) never looked back after the second roll of the dice. Paid off his $2,000 marker. Cashed in 55 BIG ONES, and still made this common and certainly ridiculous remark.

Another example took place on a 25¢ Crap Table at BENNY BINION'S HORSESHOE CASINO in downtown Vegas. (At Binion's you may make a minimum pass-line bet of 50¢, to a maximum bet of $1,000 plus TEN TIMES ODDS of $10,000.) You may even go stronger if you make arrangements with Benny Binion or one of his sons, (Jack or Teddy) or whoever is in charge at that time of day or night.

Benny the father, was once asked how big of a limit he would give Howard Hughes, should Hughes wish to shoot craps? After thinking for just a moment Benny said, he would let Hughes bet the DESERT INN on the Pass Line. Let Hughes take double odds with the SANDS and the FRONTIER, and should the Pass Line point be a 4-6-8-or 10, then Hughes could bet the CASTAWAYS and the SILVER SLIPPER on the Hard way. As for the LANDMARK?? Benny, like most oldtime classy operators, felt it only right that Hughes should have at least one joint left to get started with again. (Floating crap game operators never look to put a producing customer into bankruptcy. As long as the solid citizen is making a buck, then he is a potential long term customer. This move seems to be forgotten by some of the casino operators that look to stretch and break many of their customers.)

At Binion's it is not unheard of, for a group of hi-rollers from Texas, Hawaii or the East to phone on ahead saying they were coming in to take a shot at the Binion bankroll. These desperados usually come up with 50 or 100 BIG ONES a piece, and are fully prepared to take the Binions for one or two million.

A well known gambler, just recently beat the Binions and the Riviera Hotel for more than $1 million dollars. I was in Vegas at the time but didn't personally see this "Jimmy C." from West Texas in action. This same Jimmie C. also wanted to go into the Guinness Book of World Records, by making the LARGEST SINGLE BET on a blackjack table. It was to be ONE hand only, (win or lose) for $100,000. Jack and Teddy agreed to accept this bet, with the following conditions. Just in case . . . there would be no split or double down. Just stand or hit. He would however, in case he drew a blackjack, be paid the regular 3 to 2. Jimmie C. wasn't exactly happy about not having all the options, (double down or split) but he still accepted. He won his bet and gave the dealer a $10,000 toke. (So they said.)

As I mentioned, I was in Vegas but didn't personally see the MILLION DOLLAR WIN at the crap tables, nor the 100 BIG ONES at Blackjack. Employees at Binion's that I personally know, swear that all of this did take place. (But why Tommy, when you told me this, did you have your legs crossed??)

I won't dispute that this actually took place. I have seen some very big individual wins in the past 50 years. Mostly in the Eastern U.S. at some of the BY INVITATION ONLY private floating crap games. Five and ten thousand dollar packages of $100 bills, and even plenty of $1,000 bills (that were in circulation until not too long ago) were the common playing units. Unlike casino or most floating crap games, these special games had NO table or house limits. These boys just took their best shot, and often one or two of them would wind up with the WHOLE TEPPEL SCHMALTZ. (The woiks.)

The winner (or winners) in these games would take care of the game operator and his dealers. The operator would supply the location for the game, plus the food and beverages. (And even the access to a few 38-26-38's.) The players brought their own SECURITY with them. Please believe that I am not trying to name or number drop, when I mention certain incidents that may sound a bit like bullshalony. Newcomers to the crap game may question certain things that we say.

Those of us that have been a part of the street action crap game, know that what I am saying is quite tame compared to what has and what is right now taking place in crap games across the country. As far as Las Vegas is concerned, it's entire modern history is just over 50 years old. They have also contributed their fair share of truth and bullshalony. (Including the real or imagined "green spots" in the desert.)* The

Las Vegas definition for "green spots": Fertilized by other than animal or vegetable matter.)

And now, "LONG WINDED WILLIE" as I am occasionally called by my students, let's get back to this second "over the hump" example. Two young men put up their last $30. Bought a stack of "birds" (25¢ chips), and the balance in singles. They ran into a couple of quick miss-outs and were down to 10 or 12 dollars, when A BIG ONE started. The player member of the two pumped up his play, and when the shooter sevened out, he had $1700 in his chip rack, plus a good sized laydown on the table. What did he say?? You're right!! These two JUNIOR DEGENERATES had pooled their case money. Ran into a big hand. Locked up a fair piece of green and still didn't "GET OVER THE HUMP".

Are these two examples enough to start you thinking?? If not, there are hundreds more where they came from.

BORN LOSERS

How many times haven't you heard a crapshooter say, that all he wants to WIN (or grind out) is X numbers of dollars a day? He will very seldom (if ever) say, how much he is prepared to LOSE at any one session or day, should the dice go against him. Here is just one of the many examples I've run into. (See if it fits.)

This crapshooter had set for himself a daily win figure of $100, give or take a few dollars. He had apparently been on an extended win streak for some time, as he acted very confident, and even a bit cocky. One of the dealers had pointed him out to me and asked what I thought of his play?

His play was quite simple, and if anything, a bit weak. He would bet $10 on the Pass Line and take odds. He would then bet $10 on the Come Line and again take odds. He continued making Pass Line and Come Line bets and never increased the size of any winning bets. He kept a rough running count of his chips, and would actually walk away in the middle of a hand as soon as he had approximately the $100.

I was in the Resorts International Casino for a few days later, and saw this same player at a $25 MINIMUM BET crap table. This could mean one of two things. Either he had built up his bankroll, to where he was now going for a HIGHER daily win, or else he had hit the BRICK WALL and was chasing. Unfortunately the latter was the case. The dice had turned AGAINST him.

He wound up losing $4,000! Not $100. Not $400, but an UNBELIEVABLE $4,000!! First of all, where the hell did he get away carrying $4,000 on himself? (Yes I know he could have had it on deposit in the cashier's cage, or a credit line with the casino.) That still wasn't an answer! He only came to win $100 a day. How much did he set as his LOSS LIMIT?? His home? His business? His family? I shouldn't make it sound so surprising. I've seen it happen far too many times.

This is just one more reason why you must let your MONEY MANAGEMENT do all the guessing for you. This player's aim was to limit his winnings. This is in contrast to common sense that tells you to LIMIT YOUR LOSSES, but NEVER LIMIT YOUR WINNINGS.

There is no written guarantee that his player couldn't have left the table a $4,000 winner, instead of a $4,000 loser. Some of the unfinished hands that he walked away from when he so arrogantly announced "I'VE GOT MINE", could have been that big, or bigger. (He'll never know.) I don't take a sadistic delight in seeing setbacks happen to crapshooters. At the same time, I don't feel the least bit sorry for this type of player. His weak method of play was barely acceptable. HIS MONEY MANAGEMENT WASN'T WORTH TWO CENTS ON THE DOLLAR!!

You get NO GUARANTEE of winning even when you play CORRECTLY. But at least you play as though you DESERVE to win. Should YOU run into a hand or shoot, then I can give you a guarantee that "YOU WILL GET THE MONEY"*. (*Many times more than the average player.)

BETTING BUDDIES

A common sight at the crap tables are two or more friends or relatives playing at the SAME table. A smart move would be for them to pool their money and play at two or more tables at the the same time. This way they could have two or more chances of hitting a winning table.

This BETTING BUDDY CONCEPT could also be used by the husband and wife team. Especially since the money is usually from the same pocket. (His.) The husband and wife team could even play back to back at adjoining tables. This way they could keep in touch and if necessary, help each other. You would be pleasantly surprised at how much friction could be avoided between husband and wife, when they are BETTING BUDDIES, instead of the wife being THE GOOD LUCK CHARM, GONE BAD!! (It's ALWAYS the wife's fault??)

It's possible for three out of four members of a gambling team to be at losing tables. The fourth member of the team could be at a WINNING table, and more than overcome the losses of the other three members. At the same time, it is quite possible for two or more members to be at winning tables. You might argue that it would also be possible for all FOUR members to be at the same table, and have that table turn out to be a winning or profitable table.

Granted!! This is a crap game, where anything CAN and DOES happen. However, which of the four of you are going to HANDICAP which will be the winning table? Doing it my way, you have four chances (four crap tables) of hitting one or more profitable tables.

Two of the nicest hands I had seen in some time, took place at two adjoining tables---at almost the same time. These MONSTERS took place at tables number three and four at the RESORTS INTERNATIONAL CASINO in Atlantic City. (Table numbers have since been changed, but they are the first two tables you run into when you enter the casino from the hotel lobby entrance.)

Both of these hands started within a couple of minutes of each other. Both tables had a $25 minimum and $1,000 maximum table limit. This meant that you could bet $1,000 flat and take another $1,000 in odds. The wrong bettor could also bet $1,000 on the Don't Pass and lay enough to win another $1,000. You could also continue making Come or Don't Come bets for the same amount. Of the 16 crap tables in the casino at the time, these were the ONLY tables with a $1,000 maximum table limit. All the other tables had a $500 maximum table limit. (Except the $2 tables. They had a $200 maximum table limit.) This was unusual since the MINIMUM bet on the $1,000 tables were $25, as was the minimum bet on the tables that only had a $500 MAXIMUM limit.

Things have changed SLIGHTLY on the table limits at the Resorts International Casino. You may now (as a right bettor) bet up to $10,000 flat and take up to $30,000 in TRIPLE ODDS. The wrong bettor may also lay to win the same amounts. Not bad for a joint that has been operating against the BIG BOYS for just over 7 years. It took Las Vegas almost 50 years for one of their joints to hit these figures. (Size of bets.) BENNY BINION'S HORSESHOE CASINO was the first to openly offer them in 1982. (Binion's will give you ANY limit, providing you start OFF THE SHOULDER with your biggest bet.)

Resorts International Casino won $260,000,000 in their first full year of operation. (1978-1979) An amount unheard of in the history of LEGAL gambling.

Getting back to these TWIN MONSTER HANDS. The hand or shoot on table #3 lasted for 40 minutes of fairly fast play. The hand on the #4 table continued for almost another 30 minutes. (A total of ONE HOUR and TEN MINUTES!!)

There were at the start of these monster hands, quite a few BLACK CHECK ($100) players at both tables. The rest of them had to be at least GREEN CHECK ($25) players, as both were $25 minimum bet tables.

Before the hands or shoots at either of these tables were very far along, most of the 18 or 20 players at each table were betting black checks. A few of the more aggressive players were even into the PURPLE ($500) CHECKS. It only took a few minutes for the chip runners to start bringing "fills" (refills of chips) to both tables.

One of the Pit Bosses that I had personally known since his "break-in" days in Vegas, (I could believe his figures) told me that more than $500,000 combined, was eventually brought to the two tables. By the time both hands were with, the players had won just over $600,000. (Not bad for $1,000 Maximum Limit crap tables.)

One player who had reached the table limit in his bets, had his wife make IDENTICAL BETS. In this way they had DOUBLE the table limit in action. One of the pit bosses (not my friend) went over to this player and told him that since the money was all from ONE SOURCE, he could no longer continue making these "over the limit" bets. There was a bit of an argument for a minute or two, but since they had BOTH been playing at that table since before the hand got started, (he BLACK CHECKS, she GREEN CHECKS) the House had little choice but to sweat it out. (Too bad!! Let's hold a TAG DAY for them.)

I brought up this particular example to emphasize my point. In this case, both the husband and wife TEAM at adjoining tables, could have GOTTEN THE MONEY. As a matter of fact, it would have been a better deal, if they HAD been at adjoining tables. Their table was the one that lasted 40 minutes. I won't insult your intelligence by saying there was any way for a player to get in on the hour and ten minute hand, once it got started. They could have had them both, had they been using my BETTING

BUDDY CONCEPT, and played at BOTH of these ADJOINING TABLES.

FRINGE BENEFITS for a HIM and a HER team, could be many. One of the most painful sights at the gaming tables or race track, is to see NORMALLY CONSIDERATE couples, both young and old, tearing into each other on account of gambling reverses. (In everyday life, these couples can usually cope with their reverses.) When gambling, it's most often the man at his WORST behavior, and the blameless woman at her MOST pathetic. Occasionally you may see the opposite. This is quite uncommon, since most women (until just lately) had become accustomed to playing the part of the SCAPEGOAT to the (what has just lately become) FRUSTRATED and INSECURE male.

A man's EGO being what it is, doesn't accept being a LOSER in front of his woman. No matter how good an ACTOR he might be, he KNOWS she can read his facial expressions. This infuriates him even more! For example: at the race track, this man will tell his woman that he is going to bet on a certain horse. In the meantime, he might sneak in bets on one or more other horses. (Hi somebody we ALL know!!) Then, like the little boy he is, show (show off) her a winning ticket on a horse whose name he didn't so much as mention before the race. This CAN'T happen at the crap table. Win or lose. Smart or weak. Big or small. All of your bets are out in the open for your women, as well as the world to see.

In spite of the expected occasional setback, I still believe that a happy medium would be the BETTING BUDDY CONCEPT. Both in everyday life, as well as at the gaming tables. The expression of equality should make for an HONEST partnership between the man and his woman. As well as a TRUSTING team of players.

THE VOCAL MAJORITY (THE RIGHT BETTOR)

In the first series of plays, what you will be reading, will (for the Right Bettor) cover between 80 and 90% of all the dollar action (or betting) that takes place at the crap table. I will show you the CORRECT way of making these plays.

Whether you are a regular or an occasional player, after reading this section, you should (provided of course that you've studied and done your homework) be a knowledgeable crapshooter and money player.

One of the many FRINGE BENEFITS will be your ability to spot WEAK PLAYS and WEAK BETTORS. Spotting of weak players could affect you in two ways. (1) Be a S.O.B. and ridicule the weak player. (2) You can feel compassion and attempt to be of help. This may not prevent YOU from still making the odd foolish bet, but you will start feeling a bit simple, KNOWING that you are making a weak play.

For what it is worth, perhaps 90% of the material you read will be written by me as a crap game employee. (As a dealer, a part owner, or a full owner of a floating crap game.) The importance of this being, that in the more than 50 years (since 1929) I have been in a position to both WATCH and EVALUATE all the plays I cover. The other 10% or less, were the finishing touches to any rough edges. This I have been doing as a player since some years before 1929.

Some of my readers will benefit (financially) from these plays on their first trip to the tables. Others may not get lucky until somewheres up the road. (Unfortunately, it's still a fact that if nothing worthwhile shows on the table, then you sure as hell won't even be able to STEAL a winning bet!!)

Win or lose, you will at least know you are playing as though YOU DESERVE TO WIN. All things being equal, when something DOES show, YOU WILL GET THE MONEY. (Again I'll repeat, the expression "getting the money" in gambling jargon, means to win three, four, five or even ten times as much as the weaker player will win on the SAME HAND with the SAME INITIAL BET.)

As a member of the VOCAL MAJORITY you will share in all the excitement, that can (more than in any other form of gambling) take place at the crap table. At the race track, a group of 12 or 15 acquainted players are usually rooting for a number of different horses. After the race is over, you won't see them all with smiles on their faces. Take this same group of players to the crap table, and there's a good chance you will see all 12 or 15 of them rooting for the SAME HORSE (The SAME SHOOTER.) The crap game is the one place, where complete strangers (from a bum to a baron) can in the course of a 15 or 20 minute hand or shoot, become bosom buddies.

A most important bit of advice. PICK and STICK to the one method of play that most appeals to and excites you. PLAY FOR KEEPS!! You will stand a much better chance of walking TO the cashier's cage, rather than PAST the cashier's cage.

TEACHER OF CRAPS . . . DOCTOR OF DICE

A TEACHER OF CRAPS works with a pupil from scratch.

A DOCTOR OF DICE analyzes and recommends changes in the play of a practicing crapshooter.

As a Doctor of Dice, my method of helping a player at the crap table is quite simple. I watch my "patient" in action for 20 or 30 minutes. We then take a break and go to one of my "consulting rooms". (The COFFEE SHOP or the WHISKEY BAR.)

I will now explain to the player how, with the same size starting bet, he can financially improve ON HIS OWN METHOD OF PLAY. I won't (unless I am specifically asked to) convert or change a player's present method of play.

REASON #1 why I won't (on my own) change a player's method of play, is because THIS IS A CRAP GAME where anything can and does happen. In spite of what he may feel is right, the dice have made a liar out of your teacher (the Dice Doctor) too many times for him to continue trying to outguess them.

REASON #2 is because the player who occasionally goes to Las Vegas, Atlantic City, the Bahamas or elsewhere is usually looking for fast action. (Especially if he is with the wife or girl friend.) He has a very limited time in which to gamble. (The little lady doesn't want to know from nothing!) She came with you to have a good time. Shows, gourmet meals and hours and hours at poolside. Certainly not to stand beside you at the crap table. (Particularly should the dice turn against you, and you start glaring at YOUR GOOD LUCK CHARM GONE BAD)

Fabulous stage shows and grand gourmet meals ARE A WASTE OF TIME to most gamblers. (What gambler wants to take an hour or an hour and a half to eat one meal, when there's a chance of a big one showing while he's eating?? A piece of pie and a cup of coffee is much easier for him to digest.) As for the stage shows, quite a number of the crapshooters will put on their own DRUNK or WISE GUY SHOW. After the FINAL ACT these artists find that they have paid not only for the show, but the wages of the ACTORS and the STAGE HANDS as well.

Granted, even the drunk or loudmouth can get lucky at the crap table. THE DICE CAN'T TELL THE DIFFERENCE BETWEEN A DISGUSTING DRUNK OR A CLASSY CRAPSHOOTER!!

THE DICE DOCTOR'S BETTING RULES FOR THE RIGHT BETTOR

THESE BETTING RULES INCLUDE
MONEY MANAGEMENT
PATIENCE
SENSIBLE PROGRESSIVE BETTING
SIZE OF YOUR BETTING STAKE (in proportion to your TOTAL bankroll)
ELIGIBLE SHOOTERS
SMART USE OF (7-11) ON THE COME-OUT ROLL
SMART USE OF CRAPS ON THE COME-OUT ROLL
SMART INCREASE IN THE SIZE OF YOUR BETTING STAKES
COME BETTING VERSUS PLACE AND BUY BETTING
CONVERTING THE COME BET (something different that really works)
THERE NEVER HAS BEEN ... THERE ISN'T NOW ... THERE NEVER WILL BE ... A SYSTEM THAT CAN OVERCOME THE HOUSE EDGE AGAINST THE CRAPSHOOTER

There is however, a set of Betting Rules that when adhered to, will keep the House Edge against the player down to the least of any Casino game, excepting card casing (card counting) at blackjack or 21. Fortunately in Craps, unlike blackjack, the fact that you are facing the House Edge ALMOST 100% of the time, YOU WILL NEVER GET BARRED FOR DICE COUNTING AT THE CRAP TABLE. (My reason for saying ALMOST 100% of the time, is because THERE ACTUALLY IS ONE BET ON THE CRAP TABLE THAT IS 100% IN FAVOR OF THE PLAYER!!)

You're wrong!! It's NOT the so-called FREE ODDS BET! First of all, you must have an EVEN MONEY PAYING FLAT BET on the Pass or Don't Pass Line. The Come or Don't Come Line, before you even have the OPTION of taking or laying the ODDS. Secondly, TAKING or LAYING the odds portion of any bet, gives you no guarantee that you will win your bet.

In TAKING the odds, it is still in the House's or the Wrong Bettors favor that you will LOSE your bet. In LAYING the odds, it is in your favor (win or lose) that you will WIN your bet. Later on, I will explain how you may occasionally work this 100% (GUARANTEED TO WIN) con bet ... (IT'S PERFECTLY LEGAL.)

Getting back to the Betting Rules, YOU ELIMINATE ALL THE GUESSWORK. This includes hunches, lucky charms, prayers, vibrations (hunh?) ESP, telekinesis, etc. You the player are no more than a ROBOT that has been programmed to make certain established (and within reason) verified moves.

I included ESP, due to the controversy regarding the ability of some persons being able to come up with more right GUESSES than others. (In our case, the dice rolls.) I won't argue as to whether this is ability or PURE CHANCE. I will however point out, that since there are only 36 combinations on a pair of dice, it is not so rare for the Crapshooter to occasionally and correctly call the next roll of the dice.

I have many times had this happen to me. In contrast, I have many more times guessed wrong. I don't recommend your betting real (or spending) money on ESP or TELEKINESIS. (Let Duke University continue their experiments on ESP and telekinesis. THEY don't have to use money for their Betting Stakes.)

Should you occasionally run into one of these VISIONS, (or right guesses) just continue doing what you've always done, turn to the player next to you and say, "I JUST KNEW HE WAS GOING TO ROLL THAT NUMBER!!"

You may accept the same moral victory for performing an act of telekinesis. In our case, I think it has something to do with moving the dice with your mind. (After more than 50 years at the crap tables, I have as yet to find a game where they'll book my mind bets!!)

The dice pit personnel on the other hand, don't want to know from nothing! All they want you to do, is to pick up the dice with one hand and roll them to the opposite end of the table. They claim that this way it is only fair to the players at both ends of the table. I agree with them as to the common courtesy to all players. Unfortunately, some members of the pit personnel are so PARANOID, they are sure you must be doing something not kosher, when you play around with, or set the dice before you roll them.

To me, that's very immature on the part of the pit personnel. I don't approve of the shooter holding up a smooth running game by playing around with the dice. I also agree (from personal observation) that the dice can be slid, blanket rolled and manipulated by a PRACTICED pair of hands, which is up to the stickman, the boxman or the floorman to physically stop in time. (Or at the very least, holler "NO ROLL".) This is one of the main reasons that you will NEVER see the stickman take his eyes off the dice, once he has given them to the shooter.

Aside from these necessary precautions, and as far as I am concerned (as a former crap game operator) the player can set the dice. Kiss the dice. Play with the dice, and even rub them between his nuts. Just roll the dice 20 inches. Give me ONE BOUNCE, and I'll personally book your bets all day.

What you are reading has not been written to amuse you. There is no shortage of books and articles on gambling that amuse, rather than assist. Certain of my lines that may sound amusing, are my way of driving home a point that could help the gambler. (Or even the non-gambler.)

All I ask of the reader before he gambles HIS HARD EARNED MONEY . . HIS INHERITED MONEY . . OR HIS EMBEZZLED MONEY . . is to study thse betting rules as long as he feels is necessary. You don't have to be a math genius. Simple arithmetic will do.

The methods of play on the following page, could be of value to the . . BREAK-IN BEGINNER . . THE OCCASIONAL CRAPSHOOTER or the MATURE PROFESSIONAL.

50% PROGRESSIVE BETTING SCHEDULE
(50% IS APPROXIMATE)

PASS LINE BET	SINGLE ODDS (4-10) (5-9) (6-8)	BETTING STAKE
.75	75-1.00-1.25	20.00
1.25	1.25-1.50-1.25	27.50
1.75	1.75-2.00-2.50	42.50
2.50	2.50-2.50-2.50	50.00
3.50	3.50-4.00-5.00	85.00
5.00	5-6-5	110.00
7.00	7-8-10	170.00
10.00	10-10-10	200.00
15.00	15-20-25	400.00
25.00	25-30-25	550.00
35.00	35-40-50	850.00
50.00	50-50-50	1000.00
75.00	75-100-125	2000.00
125.00	125-150-125	2750.00
175.00	175-200-250	4250.00
250.00	250-250-250	5000.00
350.00	350-400-500	8500.00
500.00	500-600-500	11000.00
700.00	700-800-1000	17000.00
1000.00	1000-1000-1000	20000.00

PASS LINE BET	DOUBLE ODDS (4-10) (5-9) (6-8)	BETTING STAKE
5.00	10-10-10	150.00
7.00	14-14-15	220.00
10.00	20-20-25	350.00
15.00	30-30-40	550.00
25.00	50-50-50	750.00
35.00	70-70-75	1100.00
50.00	100-100-125	1750.00
75.00	150-150-150	2250.00
125.00	250-250-250	3750.00
175.00	350-350-350	5250.00
250.00	500-500-500	7500.00
350.00	700-700-750	11000.00
500.00	1000-1000-1000	15000.00
700.00	1400-1400-1500	22000.00
1000.00	2000-2000-2000	30000.00

YOUR BETTING STAKE

To give myself and any one crap table a fair chance (and not jump from table to table) I allow myself enough money to make bets on approximately 10 ELIGIBLE SHOOTERS. (I'll explain shortly who qualifies as an eligible shooter.) This is how I arrive at my BETTING STAKE. (Not my TOTAL GAMBLING BANKROLL.)

For example, let's say I'm a $5 Passline Bettor. In a SINGLE ODDS game, the most I can take in odds behind my FLAT or PASSLINE BET, is $5 behind the 4-6-8-10, or $6 behind the 5 or 9. Therefore, (unless I run into crap rolls) the most I can invest on any one shooter is $11. I multiply this $11 by 10 for a total betting stake of $110. In a DOUBLE ODDS game, the $5 Passline Bettor would (if he wished to bet double odds) require a $150 Betting Stake, consisting of 10 times $5 on the Pass Line, plus 10 times $10 in Double Odds.

The size of your any one Betting Stake, is up to you and YOUR TOTAL GAMBLING BANKROLL. The occasional player should not use more than five (5%) percent of his Total Gambling Bankroll at any single session. The number of sessions per day is up to you and your stamina. (Or whether you are with the little lady, and are limited in your gambling time.) The MATURE or PROFESSIONAL gamblers (they don't have to be told) will seldom use more than 1% or 2% of their total gambling bankroll, for a single betting stake. The size of your Betting Stake should fluctuate according to the ups and downs of your Total Gambling Bankroll. It is this use of 1 or 2% of his TOTAL gambling bankroll, that protects the professional gambler from seldom if ever, going broke. (My using of CAPITAL LETTERS is meant to emphasize points that I KNOW are important to the crapshooter. And other gamblers or businessmen.)

When the professional gambler reaches a pre-determined LIMIT in his TOTAL gambling bankroll, he will usually take any extra monies and invest in NON-GAMBLING investments. (Government bonds, term notes, properties, or endowment plans for his family. Or STRICTLY utility Blue Chips, if he wants the stock market.)

You may start with as little as a $20 betting stake at a 25¢ crap table. With a $20 betting stake, your initial or starting bet would be 75¢ plus odds. On the other hand, providing your total gambling bankroll warrants it, you may go as high as a $2,000 SINGLE ODDS, or a $2,250 DOUBLE ODDS betting stake. Your initial or strarting size bet in either case would be $75 plus single or double odds, depending on your personal choice.

With a maximum size betting stake, you would play only in casinos or floating crap games that have at least a $1,000 plus odds, Maximum Table Limit. Otherwise, you can't increase your winning bets high enough to warrant issuing that large a betting stake. In ANY game you may play at, the maximum table limit should be at least 7 or 8 times the size of your INITIAL bet.

There are, in Nevada and New Jersey, a few casinos that could warrant a larger betting stake for the hi-roller. BENNY BINION'S HORSESHOE CASINO and the GOLDEN NUGGET CASINO in Las Vegas will give any off-the-street crapshooter a higher Maximum Table Limit. There are a few others in Vegas and Atlantic City that will accommodate a known hi-roller with a higher table limit.

Check the Betting Stake Chart, and see where you FINANCIALLY and COMFORTABLY fit in. Your Betting Stake, to the last dollar is the MOST that you can possibly lose at THIS session. Your winnings are limited ONLY to the length of time your betting stake lasts, and of course, the size of Hands or Shoots you may run into.

This is just one part of your MONEY MANAGEMENT. Although many rules combine to make the successful gambler OR businessman, money management is definitely the single most important rule. Cheating on certain of your betting rules may be harmful, but cheating on your money management or money control CAN BE FATAL!!

Make just one mistake, and you'll find it quite easy to make another 21 mistakes. For example: You've set a limit on your betting stake and by mistake (more likely weakness in money management) you go into your pocket for a piece of money. After this first sick move, you won't have any trouble reaching for another piece or two, or three or more. As is quite often the case, tapping out (or going broke) is very common.

A pathetic sight at the gaming tables is the player going through every pocket in his clothing. He refuses to believe that he has "TAKEN THE STEAM" (chased his losses) and was now broke. I have even heard these sickies call for the casino security, claiming that someone had picked their pockets.

Some of them actually hope against hope that the house will reimburse them for their losses. DON'T HOLD YOUR BREATH!! (The house has heard them all.)

The casino doesn't hold a gun to your head, forcing you to gamble. Nor do they tell you HOW to gamble your money. The fact that you DON'T or WON'T prepare yourself for the gaming tables, is nobody's fault but your own.

I don't claim that there are no pickpockets, or that you can't get robbed on the street, in the parking lot or even in your hotel room. The answer to the prevention of these incidents, is to deposit your extra money in the hotel safe. Better yet, until you DO reach a little maturity at the gaming tables, leave any extra money and valuables at home or in the bank. Don't tempt fate!! YOU AIN'T READY FOR IT.

TABLE SELECTION

All crap tables in casinos having two or more tables, are numbered from #1 and up. Stags, floating crap games or one-table casinos, don't require numbers. On entering the Craps Pit area, look for the table numbers. They are usually printed on the legs or body of the table. When they are not plainly marked, just ask any dice pit employee or dealer. You may get an odd look, but don't let it bother you. You are gambling with YOUR money. We are trying to avoid as much guesswork as possible. (One part of which is not to try and HANDICAP which is a hot table.)

A few of the useless ways that players try to handicap the crap table: Lots of chips in front of the players. (No way of knowing how much they have cost the player in BUY-INS.) Lots of noise at one particular table. (A bunch of drunks hollering after every roll of the dice. WHETHER THEY WON A BET OR NOT.) Walking from table to table, trying to get the right vibrations. (WHAT THE HELL ARE RIGHT VIBRATIONS??) The dealers or pit personnel telling you that the table has been cold all day and that a hot hand is due. (BULLSHALONY!! DUE HANDS. DUE HORSES. DUE POKER HANDS OR DUE ANYTHING, CAN'T GUARANTEE YOU ONE WINNING BET.) A player who has lost 4 or 5 consecutive bets, could just as easily lose 6 or 16 consecutive bets. He has lost his first bet and could therefore bat 1000, and lose his entire Betting Stake without winning a single bet.

By starting at the #1 Table, you are letting the Dice Pit do the guessing for you. Accept the FACT that it only takes ONE roll of the dice to turn a HOT table to ICE and vice versa.

Therefore, providing it is open and in action, we go to Table #1. Otherwise we move on to Table #2 or 3 etc. The same goes for tables that are too full to get a spot. The maximum number of players varies according to the size of the table and the physical size of the players themselves. (Also whether the players are sprawled all over the table, or standing up like CRAPSHOOTERS. This is only common courtesy to your fellow player, so show a little class. MOVE YOUR ASS.) I've worked in floating crap games where we had no trouble taking care of 25 crapshooters at tables no bigger than the average sized casino crap table.

There will be those of you that will say I'm being paranoid in even making an issue over table selection. Take my word for it, that all these bits and pieces add up to the finished product. The mature. The confident. The COMFORTABLE crapshooter.

QUALIFIED SHOOTER

All Right Bettors know the feeling of running into a string of miss-outs where one shooter after the other has failed to throw even a Natural (7 or 11), let alone make a Passline Point. We must therefore have the patience to wait until a shooter DOES roll either a Natural on his come-out roll, or makes his Passline Point, before we make OUR first bet on him. He would now be what we call a QUALIFIED SHOOTER.

Granted, an eligible shooter could win his first bet. We make OUR first bet on him. He then proceeds to roll 1, 2, or 3 crap rolls, comes out on a Passline Point, and after a few more rolls of the dice, he sevens out. This is one of the chances we must take. He did win his FIRST bet, and is therefore entitled to our betting on him. We at no time double up after crap rolls. One other move that may not appeal to the majority of crapshooters, is that since a shooter MUST make a pass before we bet on him (or her)--WE AT NO TIME PERSONALLY ROLL THE DICE!! . . . One exception would be when you have a REAL GEORGE at the table.

To the player using my set of betting rules, but INSISTING on throwing the dice, I'll make one concession: Make the smallest (minimum) bet the table will allow on the Pass Line . . . take NO odds . . . should you win your bet, then go right into your regular play as a QUALIFIED SHOOTER. (I don't approve of any change in my betting rules, but knowing the weakness of human nature, I do make the odd concession.)

It takes a bit of patience waiting for a qualified shooter. At the same time, it is quite rewarding when you realize that every time a shooter sevens out, and you are not betting on him (or her) you are saving a piece of money. You and I have many times stood and watched 4 and 5 or even 10 or more consecutive shooters not so much as make their FIRST pass or Natural. Your betting stake could be pretty sick looking should this happen to you while betting on EVERY shooter.

What we are doing, is givng up the FIRST pass, in hopes of hitting the balance of a number of passes. I have found after more than 50 years as a crap game employee and as a craps player that it is to your advantage to accept what I tell you to be good advice . . . WAIT FOR A QUALIFIED SHOOTER.

One other player I WOULD approve of rolling the dice, is the woman shooter. The stickman as one of the dealers, love to announce and hustle her as the "LUCKY LADY SHOOTER." Should she put on a hand, then both she and the dealers stand a good chance of winding up with a serious piece of money in tokes. (Tips.) I'm not kidding!! I've many times seen bets made for the women shooters when they got lucky with the dice.

SENSIBLE PROGRESSIVE BETTING

It's pretty sweet when you are in action, to run into the odd big Hand or Shoot. (Or rare MONSTER of a Hand.) They are not overly common, but they DO show. I have for days gone without hitting even a mini-monster of six or seven passes. At other times I've had my share. It is nice but not necessary to have the big hands show, in order to wind up with a profit and move up the ladder on your Betting Stakes.

My method of giving your GAMBLING MONEY fair value, is as follows:

Rule #1 . . . keeping in mind the Eligible Shooter Rule, you stay at your minimum bet until YOU hit a winner. Never double up or "TAKE THE STEAM," no matter how many consecutive losing bets you may run into.

Rule #2 . . . increase each winning bet by approximately 50% plus full odds, as shown below as well as in the SENSIBLE PROGRESSIVE BETTING CHART.

I may often repeat the following, but it does bear repeating: It's heartbreaking to watch a player making $10 plus odds bets, and after a 10 pass hand is thrown, the player is STILL making $10 bets. This player has won between $225 and $250. By using OUR method of increasing his winning bets, this player, starting with the SAME $10 plus odds bet, would wind up winning almost $2000.

At the end of any second consecutive winning bet, you are a NET WINNER on this shooter. It is now the House that must "TAKE THE STEAM" and chase THEIR losses. As long as consecutive winning passes are made, you MUST increase the size of each bet until the Table Limit is reached. You would then continue making limit bets until the shooter sevens out.

INCREASE YOUR WINNING BETS PLUS ODDS AS FOLLOWS:
75¢-1.25-1.75-2.50-3.50-5-7-10-15-25-35-50-75-125-175-250-350-500-700-1000-etc.

YOUR LOCK-UP CHIPS

Following is an extended example of how you arrive at the amount that you place into the REAR or LOCK-UP PORTION of the chip rack.

We make a $5 bet on the Pass Line. The shooter rolls a 9 and we take $6 in odds behind the 9. The shooter makes the 9 and we receive a TOTAL PAYOFF of $25.

We increase our next bet on the Pass Line to $7. The shooter rolls a 6 and we take

$10 in odds behind the 6. This makes a total of $17 that we have in action on this bet. We deduct the $17 from the $25 we had received on our winning bet on the 9, leaving us with a balance of $8. It is THIS $8 that we now place into the REAR or LOCK-UP portion of our CHIP RACK. Let us continue: The shooter makes his point of 6 and we receive a total payoff of $36.

We increase our next passline bet to $10. The shooter rolls a 4 and we take $10 in odds. This leaves us with a balance of $16 from the $36 we received in winning our previous bet on the 6. It is THIS $16 that we place into the LOCK-UP portion of the CHIP RACK.

Put VERY SIMPLY--upon winning a bet and then completing the next INCREASED BET, we place whatever remains into the REAR or LOCK-UP portion of the CHIP RACK.

CRAPS ON THE COME-OUT ROLL

Should a QUALIFIED SHOOTER throw a CRAPS on his Come-out Roll, we would again make the same minimum size bet on the Pass Line.

We continue making the same size minimum bets REGARDLESS of the number of Crap Rolls that he throws. We do not "take the steam" and double up, chasing these Crap Rolls. They are on the dice, (so like it or not) learn to accept them.

On the other hand, should we have made one or more consecutive winning passes, (increasing the size of them as our SENSIBLE PROGRESSIVE BETTING CHART shows) and THEN run into a Crap Roll, we would return to our original or minimum size bet. For example: We have increased our winning bets from $10 to $15 to $25 to $35, and on the $35 bet the shooter rolls a Crap. We now back down or return to our original $10 bet and start over, hoping to again run into a string of passes. Here's a bit of a classic that I ran into.

Some time ago, while playing at the Mint in downtown Vegas, I stepped into a 19 pass hand or shoot!! A real MONSTER, wouldn't you agree?? The only problem, was that I ran into Crap Rolls exactly six times. (On the COME-OUT ROLL for a new PASS LINE POINT.) Each time I would start over again with my initial $10 bet. I still wound up with a good profit. Had this been an UNSPOILED HAND, (no craps on the come-out roll for new pass line points) I would have, by starting with the same $10 bet on the Pass Line plus $10 in odds, and increased my betting as the PROGRESSIVE BETTING CHART shows, wound up with $11,000 in winnings on this ONE hand.

You might ask why I didn't make the same size bet (after each Crap Roll) and wind up making a much bigger win on this particular hand? First of all, after literally thousands of plays, I found it financially to my advantage to back down. I also found it easier on the nerves. One such example took place at the Riviera Hotel on the Vegas Strip.

A real pretty hand was started, in that the shooter had made eight consecutive passes for me. (And himself.) I had increased my winning bets plus odds, as follows: $10-$15-$25-$35-$50-$75-$125 and $175. I made my next $250 bet on the Pass Line. The shooter rolled a Natural (7-11). I let the $500 ride as I do on any parlays starting with a Natural. Guess what? That's right!! The shooter rolled a heart breaking crap.

There were a few raised eyebrows when I made my next bet of $10 on the Pass Line. (Just a slight drop from $500 to $10 in two rolls of the dice.) The shooter then rolled another craps. I made another $10 bet. The shooter came out on a point and I took $10 in odds. After a few rolls, the shooter sevened out.

Granted, I did lose another $30 after the $500 Crap Roll, but it could have been $750, had I continued making $250 bets and taken the odds of an additional $250. Yes, it could have gone the opposite way as well. However, I still prefer backing down. To continue making the same bets after crap rolls is actually a form of chasing, and it could be possible for you to wind up a LOSER when you are already a WINNER on this shooter.

SMART USE OF NATURALS (7 or 11)

Here is what I believe to be the SMARTEST BET on the crap table!! A fairly common occurrence at the crap table is for the shooter to roll one or more NATURALS (7 or 11) on his COME-OUT ROLLS. How many players take advantage of the 7 plus a little help from his older brother. (The 11.) Very few as a whole.

Many players will PARLAY naturals when the the bets are quite small, but not as the size of the bets increase during a good Hand or Shoot. What players should accept when they make these parlays the way I recommend, is that on the SECOND HALF of the PARLAY, they can lock up the odds portion that had been earmarked for this bet, and STILL have a 3 to 1 bet going for them.

You need only to complete ONE parlay out of FOUR to break even and ONE parlay out of THREE to show a PROFIT. For example: We have a $50 Pass Line plus $50 Odds bet coming up on the next roll, making a total of $100 earmarked for this bet. The shooter rolls a Natural (7 or 11). We now have $100 on the Pass Line. Now, providing of course that it was part of a previous winning bet during this Hand or Shoot, we LOCK UP the $50 portion that had been earmarked for the ODDS. We let the $100 ride, and one of four (4) decisions can show. (1) The shooter rolls a second Natural which COMPLETE the parlay of $200 for the original $50. (2) The shooter rolls a Pass Line Point. He makes the point and the parlay is complete. (3) The shooter rolls a Pass Line Point and then sevens out. We have at least salvaged the $50 in odds. (4) The shooter rolls a Crap and we lose the $100. We must now use a portion of the $50 that we locked up, for a reduced bet on the Pass Line.

Should you be playing and betting DOUBLE or TRIPLE ODDS, you would go for a THREE BET PARLAY instead of the TWO BET PARLAY when betting SINGLE ODDS. The payoff would come to 7 to 1. As of December, 1982, several Las Vegas casinos started dealing QUINTUPLE and even 10 to 1 ODDS. (I also recommend using the parlaying of Naturals in these cases.)

For the Wrong Bettor using my main STOP LOSS MOVE, (the 7 or 11 on the come-out roll) to be able to LAY BET 5 or 10 to 1, is a fantastic break. It's geting as close as you'll ever get (outside of a man to man fade game) to a NO JUICE CRAP GAME.

INCREASING YOUR BETTING STAKE LEVEL

Since we don't add lock-up checks to our Betting Stake, (except on our last bet, if necessary) it stands to reason that little by little, the Betting Stake will go down until it is completely used up. In the meantime we hope that the lock-up checks have been growing. Should we find that we have shown ANY PROFIT on our Betting Stake, we would remain at the same table and start over again with the same size Betting Stake. (We pocket or cash in winnings.)

Should we find that we have enough (winnings and betting stake combined) to move up to our next higher Betting Stake Level, (approximately 50% increase) we do so and pocket or cash in the balance of our winnings. (Check the Betting Stake Chart for your next higher level.)

We NEVER move up more than one level at a time. (Even though there may be times when you would win enough to move up many levels.) We won it the HARD WAY, let the house try and get it back THE SAME WAY. It will give you a good feeling when you are in the driver's seat and the house is now CHASING THEIR MONEY.

Should you show a LOSS (go drop dead) on your Betting Stake, then you would move on to the next table and start over again at your LOWEST LEVEL according to your NEW TOTAL GAMBLING BANKROLL.

I recommend 5% of your Total Gambling Bankroll for the occasional player. For the regular or professonal player, 1 or 2% is enough for any one STARTING Betting Stake. Never be afraid or embarrassed to back down when the dice are going against you. I guarantee that you will move up fast enough when the dice start moving FOR YOU. I say this not only as a player, but also as a former employee and owner of floating crap games. (Where a player sees only his own plays at the table, an employee can see the moves made by all the players.)

Believe me children, I've seen case money turn around and make a chump out of a champ.* (*Beat the House for serious money when the dice turned in the right direction for the ALMOST KNOCKED OUT player.)

BOOK YOUR OWN INSURANCE BETS!!
(the "ANY CRAPS" bet)

One of the sweetest sounds to the ears of the crap game operator, is to hear the crapshooter call "ANY CRAPS."

This player is not giving the house it's rightful commission or vigorish of 1.4% or less that it is entitled to for giving you a casino or a floating crap game in which to play. Instead, this player is giving up a whopping 11% every time he throws a piece of money to the stickman and calls "ANY CRAPS." When a player makes this "any craps" bet, he as much as says that for every eight of these bets he makes for himself, he will make the 9th bet for the House. Like it or not, this is exactly what you ar doing!!

Would you pay out $111 in premiums for every $1000 worth of merchandise or life insurance?? Not very likely, unless you were TERMINAL or that you had arranged a CANDELABRA (bonfire) JOB for the merchandise.

The "any craps" bet is the biggest (silent) money maker, of any of the proposition bets. (FOR THE HOUSE.)

When you play the Pass or Don't Pass Lines plus odds, the Come or Don't Come Lines plus odds, you ar giving up less than a 1% edge. Isn't it an insult to your own intelligence to give the house more than 11 times as much?? Want some good (honest) advice? BOOK YOUR OWN (any craps) INSURANCE BETS!!

FREE ODDS?? WHO'S KIDDING WHO??

Somewhere in the history of the LAS VEGAS STYLE crap game, some smart operator hired a MADISON AVENUE CON ARTIST to come up with a sales pitch that would use the word FREE, when publicizing the BANK or CASINO STYLE crap game.

I don't know, nor does it much matter who started this bullshalony about the so-called FREE ODDS. Even though some of us crapshooters may not academically be overly educated, we do have enough "streets smarts" to know that NOTHING is free in the (legal) Casino, or the (illegal) floating style BANK CRAPS GAME. (Except the COMPS that are semi-free. They have strings attached.)

In Army craps, stag craps or any of the other man-to-man fading crap games?? YES!! The odds could be FREE. In any of these games, it is not necessary to have a FLAT BET (that pays EVEN MONEY) in order to have THE OPTION of taking or laying the odds. (Providing of course, that another player wants to book your action.)

On the other hand, in ANY form of bank craps, (casino, floating or O.K.'d by the MAN*, *payoff crap games) you must either have that even-money flat bet, or else pay the 5% commission (or vigorish or juice) before you may if you wish (depending on which way you are betting) take or lay the odds.

And so, my fellow dice authorities?? Don't you think it's about time that you stopped conning John Q. Public into believing they're getting something "FREE" when they take or lay the odds??

Except on my PARLAY moves on NATURALS or LIVE CRAP ROLLS, you may bet your sweet life that I recommend your taking or laying the odds!! You've certainly paid for the privilege!!

As a Right Bettor, once you've missed your chance of an INSTANT WIN by catching a NATURAL (7 or 11), or an INSTANT LOSS on a Craps Roll (2, or 3 or 12) on your COME-OUT ROLL for a Pass-line Point, you are the 6/5 or 3/2 or 2/1 underdog. Now, at least scare the House a little by taking as much odds as they will allow. (Even though the House knows that they are favored to win your bet, let them worry as to how much they might have to pay out, should YOU win the bet.)

As for the Wrong Bettor; Once you've avoided the SHERIFF (the 7) or his Deputy (the 11), on the Come-Out Roll, YOU are now (win or lose) a favorite to win your bet. Stick it to them and lay ALL the odds that the joint will allow. They know you've got THEM by the nuts, so make them suffer!! (At least till a decision is reached.)

The Crap Table Crew is warned, with pain of expulsion, (or worse) not to recommend to the players, the taking or laying of odds. It is up to you, (the player) to take care of it. The dealer must however, (when asked by the player) tell him (or her) the least or the most odds you may take or lay.

By playing correctly or as I like to say, "FOR KEEPS", you will at least earn the respect of the Dice Pit Personnel. And just maybe, (if the big hand or shoot or MONSTER shows) even scare the hell out of them.

Personally, I don't want either their respect OR their condolences. I JUST WANT THEIR MONEY!! (Plus any "COMPS" for giving my action to THEM instead of to the joint NEXT DOOR.)

THE HOUSE'S HUSTLING or TOUTING BETS

The following are the House's HUSTLING or TOUTING BETS. They are of little value to the Crapshooter. The only possible value they might have, is to remind the IDIOT BETTOR of all the different IDIOT BETS that he, THE IDIOT BETTOR can make.

Before the Come-out roll for a Pass-line Point the stickman will hustle or tout the 7 and 11, or any craps, or the hi-low or horn bets.

After a Pass-line Point is established, the stickman will hustle (or recommend--as he would rather you say) the opposite. Such as the 6 opposite the 8. The 5 opposite the 9. The 4 opposite the 10, or vice versa.

In the case where the Pass-line Point being a 4-6-8 or a 10, the stickman will tout the HARDWAYS. The point must be made in pairs, such as 2-2, 3-3, 4-4, or 5-5. Made in any other way, or if a seven (7) shows FIRST you lose your bet.

These Proposition Bets on the XMAS TREE LAYOUT are a real gravy train for the House. On these ONE ROLL proposition bets, or the ALL DAY hardway bets, you the player are giving up from more than 9% to almost 17%. On the opposite bets, you are giving up between 1½% to 6²/³%, or 5% when you BUY BET the box numbers (4-5-6-8-9-10).

These expensive (for the player) bets are in contrast to the 4/5 of 1% (SINGLE ODDS) that we give up the House when we "PLAY FOR KEEPS" as we do in our recommended plays for the RIGHT or the WRONG bettor.

Should you in spite of what I have told you, still insist on making one or more of these IDIOT BETS, then at least follow my suggestions on how to bet like an INTELLIGENT IDIOT.

The weak, the stupid or the idiot bettor, will increase his winning bets as follows. (All the following bets start with $5 bets.) You may start with whatever amount that you care to lose. (Or win??)

You say that I'm being sarcastic again?? You can bet your sweet life that I am!! Nobody held a gun to your head and forced you to buy my book. (You got yourself $100,000 worth of Crap Table advice for a lousy few bucks, or it's quite possible that I "comped" you with a book.) Just be thankful that I made mine, and took the time off to write these honest pieces of advice. Now you take 50 years . . . er . . . I mean 50 hours of YOUR time to study what I've written. Perhaps you'll get yours, or at WORST, salvage some losses. (Mentally as well as financially.)

Show me a gambler who can manage his money. I'll show you a SUCCESSFUL BUSINESSMAN. Show me a gambler that won't TAKE THE STEAM AND CHASE, and I'll show you a HEART or BRAIN SURGEON who doesn't have to worry about a patient asking for a SECOND OPINION. Show me a gambler who can intelligently increase his winning bets, and I'll show you a man (or woman) with the ability to expand their own business endeavors.

HOW THE INTELLIGENT IDIOT SHOULD INCREASE HIS WINNING BETS

ANY CRAPS (1-1, 1-2, 6-6) pays 8 for 1.
 Increase as follows: 5-20-80-table limit. Continue making table limit bets.
ELEVEN (6-5) pays 15 to 1, or 15 for 1 . . . Depending on casino.
 Increase as follows: 5-40-table limit. Continue table limit bets.
SEVEN (1-6, 2-5, 3-4) pays 5 for 1.
 Increase winning bets as follows: 5-10-25-50-100-250-table limit. Continue table limit bets.
HI or LO (1-1, 6-6) pays 30 to 1, or 30 for 1. (Depending on casino). Bet one or the other.
 Increase winning bets as follows: 5-75-table limit, etc. . etc.
HI and LO (1-1, 6-6). Bet both and increase winning bets on BOTH as follows:
 5-40-table limit. Continue betting table limit.
HORN BETS (1-1, 6-6) pays 30 to 1 or 30 for 1. (1-2, 6-5) pays 15 to 1 or 15 for 1.
 Increase winning bets on ALL numbers as follows:
 5-10-20-40-80-table limit. Continue table limit bets.
HARDWAY 4 or 10 (2-2, 5-5) pays 8 for 1. Play one or both.   Increase WINNING BETS ONLY as follows: 5-20-80-table limit. Continue betting table limit.
 HARDWAY 6 or 8 (3-3, 4-4) pays 10 for 1. Play one or both.
Increase WINNING BETS ONLY as follows: 5-25-125-table limit. Continue limit bets.

If your play is so weak that you must make these bets, then it's possible that my recommending THESE increases in winning bets may just help you find YOUR needle in a haystack. Keep in mind that this is a crap game where anything can and does happen. $1 can become $1,000 in three rolls of the dice. Three consecutive HARDWAY 6's or 8's, when PARLAYED will pay you $1,000 for a $1 bill. WE'VE ALL SEEN IT HAPPEN! RIGHT?? RIGHT!!

P.S. . . . You will NEVER hear the stickman tell the players to take or lay the odds. There is NO edge in this bet for the House. Most casinos and floating crap game operators, make it hard on any dealers who even recommend these odds bets to the players. In some cases, it has cost them their job.

THE WORLD'S BEST METHOD OF PLAY FOR THE FIELD BETTOR
(INFLATED RETAIL VALUE 98¢)

To say I am embarrassed by starting out my different Methods of Play, with one that gives the House an Edge of 2.7% is putting it mildly. I begrudge the House an Edge of 3/5 or 4/5 of 1% that most of my plays cost . . . So why the FIELD BET??

Because HUMAN NATURE that includes ignorance, laziness or inability to count from 1 to 10, are the main reasons why so many dice players try to SECOND GUESS the FIELD.

For the House, it is NOT ignorance, laziness OR simple arithmetic. It is SALESMANSHIP. There is more layout space devoted to the field bet, than to most of the other proposition bets COMBINED. (In spite of what I say about field bets being such a weak bet, I have seen wins of $25,000 and even $50,000 made in FIELD BETTING.)

I have in my time as a dealer and as a player, seen more than 20 consecutive field numbers rolled. I have also, during the same time seen MORE than 20 consecutive numbers rolled without even a SINGLE field number.

In my Method of Play for the Field Bettor, should YOU run into 20 consecutive rolls of the dice without a single field number showing, you would only lose PEANUTS. Should you on the other hand, WIN 20 or more consecutive field bets, then take my word for it MR. or MRS., that starting with a $2 bill, you could wind up beating the joint for over $5,000. (I haven't as yet seen a $2 bettor make this big a win, but I have seen it done by a couple of $5 bettors.)

You might ask why, if this bet has such a potential, then how come I knock it? To be honest with you, it galls me to give the House a 2.7% edge, when I am not overly happy about giving them 1/3rd or less as much edge. The play is so simple, that my daughter Marnie learned this play when she was 7 years old. (At home of course.) She just recently turned 24.

THE BETTING RULES FOR THIS FIELD PLAY ARE AS FOLLOWS

(1) Find a casino that pays 2 to 1 on the two ACES and 3 to 1 on the two SIXES. (These are the odds paid on Field Bets in downtown Las Vegas.) All the Casinos on the Las Vegas Strip pay 2 to 1 on BOTH the 2 aces or 2 sixes, which gives them a 5.5% House Edge instead of a 2.7% House Edge that the 3 to 1 on the two sixes would be.

In Atlantic City, ALL the Casinos EXCEPTING Caesars Boardwalk Regency (so far) pays 2 to 1 on the two Aces or the two Sixes. (Caesars pays 3 to 1 on the two sixes.)

If in Northern Nevada or other areas where they pay 3 to 1 on the TWO ACES, then just play the same way. Forget this or any other Field Betting Play if you can't get these payoffs on the Field Bet. (Let them go to work.)

(2) Your starting Betting Stakes are as follows:

The $2 bettor requires a Betting Stake of $100. This $100 allows you to make 50 STARTING BETS of $2 each. Get a stack of $1 chips and the balance in $5 chips.

The $5 bettor requires a Betting Stake of $250. Get a stack of $1 chips and the balance in $5 and $25 chips.

The $25 bettor requires a Betting Stake of $1250. Get a stack of $5 chips, and the balance in $25 and $100 chips. This Betting Stake is plenty big enough for any Field Bettor. You'll make a FAIR DAY'S WAGES. (If you win.)

One FIELD BETTOR at Binion's Horseshoe Casino in Downtown Vegas was at the bar opposite the Crap Tables. (Drinks are 50¢ at Binion's.) Every so often this field bettor would take 10 $1000 YELLOW CHIPS and bet them on the field for ONE roll. (Win or lose.) He would then return to the bar for another 50¢ drink. How did he wind up with his $10,000 bets? I don't know. I got sick to my stomach just watching!! I was told later that he was at one time up over $150,000 and then blew it all back...PLUS.

(3) Place your Betting Stake in the FRONT PORTION of your Check Rack.

(4) The following is an extended example of the FIELD PLAY: You bet $2 in the field, and the shooter rolls a field number. You now have $4. Your next bet is $3 and you place the remaining $1 in the REAR or LOCK-UP PORTION of the Check Rack. The shooter again rolls a Field number and you now have $6. You increase you next bet to $5 and place the remaining $1 into the Lock-up rack. Increase each winning bet by approximately 50% as follows:

2-3-5-7-10-15-25-35-50-75-125-175-250-350-500-700-1000-etc.

(5) Should you occasionally run into 2 aces or 2 sixes, then you would accept these rolls as BONUSES and place them into the LOCK-UP RACK. For example: Your bet is $5 and the shooter rolls 2 aces that pays 2 to 1, or 2 sixes that pays 3 to 1. Your next increased bet would be $7 and you place the remaining $8 or $13 (depending) into the LOCK-UP PORTION of the Chip Rack.

(6) When you've played out your $100 Betting Stake, you take a count of the checks in your lock-up rack. Should you find that you have a TOTAL of anywheres between $101 and $149, you would again place $100 of it into the FRONT or BETTING PORTION of the Chip Rack, and start over again with the same $2 bets. You would pocket or cash in the winnings. Should you on taking a count, find that you have $150 or more, you would place the $150 into the Front or Betting Portion of the Chip Rack. Your starting bet would now be $3 instead of the $2 starting bet you had with the $100 Betting Stake. (You pocket or cash in anything you have over the $150.) You NEVER move up more than ONE Betting Level at a time!! Let the House "TAKE THE STEAM" and chase THEIR money. YOU PLAY FOR KEEPS!!

Should you show a LOSS on your $100 (or whatever) Betting Stake, you would move on to the next table, and start over again with YOUR MINIMUM BETTING STAKE.

BETTING RULES FOR THE COME LINE BETTOR

Previously I gave you a list of bets that I call BAD BETS because of the extra House Edge you must pay when you make them. I included COME BETS in this list, and in the way they are mistakenly compared to PASS LINE BETS in their entirety. Having explained the reasons why, I would therefore have to call them a "second cousin" to a bad bet.

Before I go into the Betting Rules for the COME BETTOR, I must point out that the worst move a Come Bettor can make is to spread himself out on too many Come Bets. In this case it would take many number rolls to just get back his investment on this shooter. Let alone show a profit.

Long winded hands are not overly common. The seven (7), the FRIEND of the Pass Line Bettor (on his come-out rolls) is the ENEMY of the Come Line Bettor. The Pass Line Bettor can win any number of bets when the 7 is rolled at the RIGHT TIME. The Come Line Bettor can only win ONE part bet on the 7, and that can only be on the seven-out roll, which means that the hand or shoot is at an end. (And then only if he is on the Come Line for that ONE roll. A VERY SMALL CONSOLATION PRIZE.)

The ideal for the crapshooter wanting more than just a Pass Line bet in action, is in adding ONE come bet. The Come or Flat Portion of one come bet can usually (not always) be overcome when the 7 shows on the Come-out Roll for a NEW passline Point. I won't bend or approve of more than this one come bet. Even though I've seen literally thousands of profitable Come Hands in action, I have unfortunately seen by far, MANY MORE COME BETS GO DOWN THE DRAIN.

Should you insist on making a SECOND Come Bet, then you are on your own. At least use my Betting Rules for the Come Bettor. Should you be foolish enough to want MORE than two Come Bets, then you had better find yourself another "doctor" and get A SECOND OPINION. Personally it would be an INSULT to both yours and my intelligence to consider such betting. (With dumb luck, you could possibly run into the odd big Come Hand or Shoot which would work on ALL six numbers or Come Bets. It's STILL dumb betting, and you would certainly need the luck.)

In spite of the way I feel about Come Bets, as well as ANY bet other than the Pass Line Bet, the Don't Pass Bet and Don't Come Bet, I would definitely take the Come Bets in preference to the Place or Buy Bets. In making the Come Bets, the dice do ALL THE GUESSING for me. I trust the dice rolls rather than the player's handicapping or guessing of which number or numbers to play. IT'S MUCH EASIER ON THE NERVES!!

You may counter by saying that in Place or Buy Betting, you would win a bet after your number shows for the FIRST time, but in Come Betting your number must show TWICE for you to win your bet. True . . . but at least the Come Bet number DID show ONCE, and it must show for that first time before it can possibly show for a second time. The Place or Buy numbers that YOU select, may not show ANYTIME that you are on them.

In all cases, it's the dice and not the player that you depend on to guess right. It is also for this reason that I strongly emphasize the FUTILITY of trying to HANDICAP THE CRAP TABLE. This includes the CRAPSHOOTERS and the BOX NUMBERS. This is not a horse race where there is the help of a trainer, a jockey, plus the past performances which could possibly (not definitely) help a horse win a race.

The dice on the other hand, are on their own. THERE IS NOT A THING THAT THE CRAPSHOOTER CAN DO TO CONTROL THE OUTCOME OF EVEN ONE DICE ROLL! (Excluding FUNNY dice or SPIN THROWS by trained people.)

CORRECT MOVES FOR THE COME BETTOR

(1) Wait for a QUALIFIED SHOOTER.

(2) Make your Pass Line Bet. (At all times follow the rules outlined for the PASS LINE BETTOR.)

(3) Make your Come Bet. Should a box number (4-5-6-8-9-10) show, you would take the odds.

(4) Should the seven show, then naturally the Hand or Shoot is finished.

(5) Should one or more consecutive Crap Rolls show on your initial or minimum Come Bet, you would continue making MINIMUM Come Bets. (You would NEVER double up in an effort to catch up.)

(6) Should you have had one or more INCREASED winning Come Bets and then run into a Crap Roll, you would BACK DOWN or return to your original minimum bet. (In other words, you are following ALL the Pass Line Betting Rules. This includes the Parlay on Naturals. Since there is NO possibility of TWO sevens showing on the Come Line, it is then understandable that a COME LINE PARLAY must start with an ELEVEN (11).)

(7) Increase your winning Come Bets the same as you do your Pass Line Bets. I know that I am continually repeating myself!! It is better I tell you the same thing 20 TIMES till you get it straight. Your kindergarten teacher did the SAME THING. Since many of my pupils are in the SAME class, it can't HOIT!! I wish it had been this easy AND this cheap for me to learn craps.

I'll concede there will be the occasional Multi-number Hand or Shoot where the seven will STAY AWAY. The Come Line Bettor will win bet after bet. The Pass-line Bettor, on the other hand may not even win his first bet on the Pass Line. In spite of this, I assure you that BET FOR BET, and DOLLAR FOR DOLLAR, the Pass Line Bet will in THE LONG RUN far exceed the winning bets on any individual Come Bets.

The $5 Pass-line Bettor taking SINGLE ODDS and ONE Come Bet, would require a $220 Betting Stake. With TWO Come Bets $330. The $5 Pass-line Bettor taking DOUBLE ODDS and ONE Come Bet, would require a $300 Betting Stake. With TWO Come Bets $450.

The $25 Pass-line Bettor taking SINGLE ODDS and ONE Come Bet, would require an $1150 Betting Stake. With TWO Come Bets $1750. The $25 Pass-line Bettor taking DOUBLE ODDS and ONE Come Bet, would require a $1650 Betting Stake. With TWO Come Bets $2550. Multiply the $5 Pass-line Bettor's numbers to get at YOUR Betting Stake.

CONVERTING THE COME BET

Before I show you how to CONVERT the COME BET, let me first explain the difference between the EASTERN or 5% CRAPS LAYOUT as originally played in the Eastern U.S., the Bahamas, other Caribbean Island Casinos and elsewhere, and the more popular LAS VEGAS CRAPS LAYOUT, as is used in Nevada, New Jersey, most floating crap games, etc. (And just lately being used in many island casinos.)

Anyone who had played craps in the Bahamas, knows that until lately there was NO Come Betting Line, nor a Don't Come Line on their craps layout. Aside from the Pass Line or Don't Pass Line, any numbers you wanted to bet on or against, required that you pay a 5% commission.

For the crapshooter using my BASIC STRATEGY PLAY for either the RIGHT or the WRONG BETTOR, this 5% BLACKMAIL would not affect you. For the crapshooter who wished to bet on or against OTHER NUMBERS, this 5% game compared to the Las Vegas game, is a hard nut to crack. (In plain English, THEY'VE GOT YOU BY THE NUTS!!)

It had bugged me for many years, that all bets EXCEPTING the Pass Line, the Don't Pass Line or the Don't Come Line plus odds, COULD BE FAULTED. (For previously explained reasons, this also included the COME BETS.) Granted, the Come Bet has MORE MERIT than the Place or Buy Bets. That doesn't mean there couldn't be an even better alternative, by COMBINING the advantages of the Come Bet together with the Place or Buy Bet.

It was this CONVERTING or COMBINING that I can thank the Bahamas for. The fact that there was NO Come Betting Line (at the time) on the Bahamas Craps Layout, made it easier for me to come up with the answers.

This Converting of the Come Bet can be played WITH or WITHOUT the Pass Line Bet. (As can ANY of the plays that I have written up for the RIGHT BETTOR.) However, as in all my plays for the Right Bettor, the Pass Line part of the play is to me, not only the key to most of the moves, but MY BIGGEST MONEY MAKER as well. In this play as in all plays which include the Pass Line Bet, you will adhere to all the Betting Rules outlined in my BASIC STRATEGY FOR THE RIGHT BETTOR.

As is usual, our first move is deciding on the size of our Betting Stake. There will be a difference in the totals required for the Bahamas (or Eastern) Layout and the Las Vegas Layout.

On the Las Vegas layout, the player making a $5 plus SINGLE ODDS Pass Line Bet, plus two (2) CONVERTED COME BETS, would require a Betting Stake of $350. On the Bahamas Layout, the player would require a Betting Stake of $320. The reason for the difference is that in the Bahamas you would BUY BET the 6 and 8 for $10 each, plus the 5% commission charge. On the Las Vegas Layout, you would PLACE BET the 6 and 8 for $12 each. Thereby making a differnce of $30 on your Betting Stake. On the Vegas Layout, the $25 Bettor would require a $1750 Betting Stake.

(I'll repeat.) We will be working with three (3) separate bets. The Pass Line plus odds Bets, and two (2) Converted Come Line Bets. The individual totals of each of the three bets will be approximately the same size. This is as it should be. You don't HANDICAP or favor ONE number to be better than any of the other numbers. Over the short period of time that the occasional player is in action, a 4 or a 10, a 6 or an 8 can quite easily average out to where one will show as often as the other.

You will quite often see a player bet $60 each on the 6 and 8. $25 each on the 5 and 9, and as much or LESS on the 4 and 10. Granted, on a pair of dice, there are more 6's and 8's than there are 5's and 9's, and there are more 5's and 9's than there are 4's and 10's. These crapshooters are betting on the LAW OF AVERAGES.

This is fine, and might possibly work out . . . if . . . the player could live 328 years and roll the dice a few million times. Unfortunately we 50 year TEMPORARY CRAP TABLE TOURISTS have to depend a little more on the Law of Probabilities. How many times haven't you seen the OUTSIDE NUMBERS (4-5-9-10) show in bunches, where on the other hand you couldn't STEAL a bet on the 6 or 8??

In other words, FORGET the Law of Averages. The House must and does work with this law, THEY BOOK ALL BETS. Once in awhile, even THEY get double-crossed by the cards or the dice. Let your Money Management and Total Gambling Bankroll tell you the size of your bets. Let the rolls of the dice HANDICAP the numbers that you will bet on. (The dice may only be a pair of lifeless cubes, but they are still smarter than we are. I would just as soon let them tell me what to do.)

O.K. children! Let's get on with the moves in this play. It's a bit tricky but if it's ACTION you want without going nuts, then this play fills the bill.

(1) Wait for a QUALIFIED SHOOTER, then make a $5 bet on the Pass Line. The shooter rolls a 4 and you take $5 in odds.

(2) Now instead of making a $5 bet on the Come Line, you WAIT for the shooter to roll a point, and THEN make a PLACE or BUY BET on the number that has been rolled. The shooter rolls a 5 and we make a $10 PLACE BET on the 5. We now wait for the shooter to roll a second number. He comes out on a 6 and we PLACE BET the 6 for $12. (On the the Eastern Craps Layout, we would have to BUY BET both the 5 and the 6 for $10 each.)

(3) The shooter rolls a 5 and we receive $14. We still have a $10 bet on the 5. We increase the $10 bet on the 5 to $15, and place the REMAINING $9 into the REAR or LOCK-UP PORTION of the CHIP RACK. The shooter rolls another 5, and we receive a $21 payoff. We increase the $15 Place Bet on the 5 to $25, and place the remaining $11 into the lock-up rack. The shooter rolls a 6 and we receive $14. We increase the $12 PLACE BET on the 6 to $18, and place the REMAINING $8 into the LOCK-UP RACK. The shooter rolls another 6 and we receive a $21 payoff. We increase the $18 Place Bet on the 6 to $30 and place the remaining $9 in the lock-up rack. The shooter rolls a 4, and we win our Pass Line Bet. We receive a total payoff of $25.

(4) We now increase our Pass Line Bet to $7, and the shooter rolls an eleven (11). We now have $14 on the Pass Line. We PARLAY (or let ride) the entire $14, and the shooter rolls an 8. As in our Basic Strategy Betting Rules for the Right Bettor, we do NOT take any odds behind the Pass Line Bet WHEN WE HAVE A PARLAY WORKING. We now lock up the REMAINING $18 from the $25 we had received when we made our FIRST Pass Line Point of 4. The shooter makes his Pass Line Point of 8 and OUR PARLAY IS NOW COMPLETE. We receive $28 for our original $7 bet.

Our next increased Pass Line Bet is $10. (Our increased winning bets on the Place and Buy Bets, as well as our Pass Line Bets are approximately 50%.) The shooter rolls a 5. We take down (have the Dealer return to us) the $25 we had Place Bet on the 5. We take $10 from this $25 and place it behind the Pass Line point of 5 as odds.

Had we NOT shown an increase on the Place Bet that we had on the 5, and then have it become the Pass Line Point, we would have returned the $10 Place Bet to the Betting Stake Portion of the Chip Rack. (In other words, if a Place or Buy Bet DOES NOT make money for you, then you DO NOT put it into the lock-up rack.) We now wait for the shooter to roll a number before we make another Converted Come Bet. The shooter rolls a Craps. In normal Come Betting you would have lost the Flat Portion of your Come Bet. (Or approximately half of a full SINGLE ODDS Come Bet.) In our CONVERTING of the Come Bet, we can roll craps all day, without losing a chip.

The shooter now rolls an eleven (11). In normal Come Betting you would have doubled your bet and had a Parlay started. In CONVERTED Come Betting, you do not win anything. This is a DISADVANTAGE for Converted Come Betting. However, you and I know that there are FOUR (4) ways in which a Craps Roll can be made, and only TWO (2) ways in which an eleven can be made. Therefore, the Converted Come Bet has a two to one advantage on Craps Rolls versus the Eleven.

The shooter again rolls the dice, and comes out on a 6. Now here it gets a bit tricky. Since we have established a Pass Line Point, this 6 now becomes the Converted Come Bet, and since we ALREADY have a 6 as a Converted Come Bet, here is what we must do: First of all, the dealer pays us off on the $30 Place Bet we have working on the 6. This payoff is $35. At the same time, we have the dealer reduce the $30 Place Bet on the 6 to $12. (This was another STOP LOSS move in the Converting of Come Bets.) It is by coincidence (on purpose) that the 6 showed up instead of another box number. It is when this happens that it gets just a bit confusing. WHAT DID YOU EXPECT . . . EVERYTHING FOR NOTHING??

We are now holding in our hands the chips from three different sources. (A) We have $18 remaining from our completed $28 parlay. (B) We have $15 remaining from the $25 Place Bet that we had on the 5, when it became our Pass Line Point. (C) We have $35 from the $30 Place Bet on the 6, plus another $18 which remained when we reduced that SAME $30 Place Bet to $12. We must still wait for another Converted Come Bet to show before we place whatever remains into the lock-up rack. The shooter rolls a 9, and we Place Bet the 9 for $10. And now children, you tell me, how much we must place into the lock-up rack? (If your answer is ¼#$¢&%*.?, then you are right!!)

The shooter rolls the dice a number of times. Our Place Bets on the 6 and 9 are rolled a few times and are increased to $60 on the 6 and $50 on the 9. (As long as we are making mind bets, we might as well show a profit.) The shooter makes his Pass Line Point of 5, and we receive a total payoff of $45.

(5) Our next increased Pass Line Bet is $15. The shooter rolls a crap, (1-1, 1-2, 6-6). In normal Pass Line Betting, should we come out on a crap roll, on our minimum bet, we would again make a minimum size bet. On the other hand, should we have had one or more consecutive increased wins, and THEN come out on a Crap Roll, we would back down to our ORIGINAL minimum size bet. (In our case $5.) We do the same thing now. At the same time, we would take down (have the dealer return to us) all Place or Buy bets, and start over again with two NEW converted Come Bets. (Also at their minimum size.) Should we have shown a PROFIT on any of the bets we had taken down, we would place the entire amount into the lock-up portion of our chip rack. Otherwise, we would replace them into the betting portion of the chip rack.

Here is another advantage in Converting the Come Bet over the NORMAL Come Bet. In normal Come Betting the FLAT or Come Line Portion pays EVEN MONEY. Only the Odds Portion pays the TRUE ODDS. In the CONVERTED Come Bet, the ENTIRE BET pays either Place Bet Odds, or in the case of the 4 or 10, pays the TRUE ODDS by paying the 5% Buy Bet commission. For example: You make a NORMAL Single Odds Come Bet of $25 and the shooter rolls a 10. You take $25 in odds. This makes a total of $50 that you have invested on this Come Bet. The shooter makes the 10 and you receive a payoff of $125.

We now make the same bet by CONVERTING the Come Bet. We WAIT until the shooter rolls the 10. We can now either Place Bet the 10 for $50, or by paying an extra $2 commission, Buy Bet the 10 for $50. On the shooter making the 10, we would on the Place Bet receive a total payoff of $140. On the Buy Bet, we would receive a total payoff of $150. (Most casinos and floating crap games will permit you to make a $50 Buy Bet for $2. BENNY BINION'S HORSESHOE CASINO in downtown Las Vegas, is the only casino in the world that won't charge you anything . . . UNLESS YOU WIN YOUR BET.)

On the VEGAS CRAPS LAYOUT, you should BUY BET the 4 and 10 ONLY. It is to your advantage to PLACE BET the INSIDE NUMBERS (5-6-8-9).

Unfortunately, on the EASTERN CRAPS LAYOUT, you must BUY BET any of the numbers that you care to bet on.

THE 6 AND 8 PLAY FOR THE RIGHT BETTOR

(Almost) One hundred per cent of all writers on the game of craps, will tell you that your BEST BETS are the Pass Line, the Don't Pass Line, the Come Bet Line and the Don't Come Bet Line. Without taking or laying ANY ODDS, the House Edge against you is betwen 1.402% and 1.414%. By taking or laying the SINGLE ODDS, the House Edge is cut to about 4/5 of 1%. By taking or laying DOUBLE ODDS, the House Edge is about 3/5 of 1%. By taking or laying TRIPLE ODDS, the House Edge is down to 2/5 of 1%. Yes. They are even dealing QUINTUPLE ODDS, and believe it or not, 10 TIMES ODDS at BENNY BINION'S HORSESHOE CASINO in downtown Las Vegas. The MINIMUM bet at Binion's is 50¢. The MAXIMUM bet is as high as you care to arrange. (Tommy told me that they may have to go back to QUINTUPLE or 5 to 1 ODDS.) Too many Pass Line and Come Line Bettors are betting the equivalent of $1 Flat, and taking $10 in Odds. For the Wrong Bettors, the 10 to 1 odds is getting very close to a NO JUICE GAME!! So much for the Odds and House Edge Trivia. Let's get on with the 6 and 8 play.

Ninety-nine per cent of the same writers will tell you that the NEXT best bet is in PLACE BETTING the 6 and 8. (If these writers would change the wording to read LEAST WORST BET, then I would probably join them to make it read, 100% of all (dice) writers.)

They compare the 6 and 8 House Edge of 1.51% to the 1.402% and 1.414% FLAT PORTION of the Pass or Don't Pass, the Come or Don't Come House Edge. These writers either DON'T KNOW or they forget to tell you, that in casino or bank craps, (legal or otherwise) these Right or Wrong bets are INCOMPLETE BETS until the ODDS PORTION has been LAYED or TAKEN. Thereby cutting the House Edge against you down to 2/5 or 3/5 or 4/5 or less of 1%. Now, don't you see why the dealers or the boxmen won't TOUT or HUSTLE you into taking or laying the odds?? There's NOTHING in it for the House. Here's another way you may look at it. You've paid the rent by making a Pass Line Bet that pays EVEN MONEY. Why shouldn't you (in effect) use the room. (Or take the odds??) This portion of the bet pays the TRUE ODDS that you are entitled to.

Place Betting the 6 or 8 are COMPLETE BETS in themselves, no matter how big or small they may be. They are still 1.51% against you, which is almost as much or more than DOUBLE the House Edge of the COMPLETED Right or Wrong bet. There are NO INCOMPLETE or PARTIAL PLACE BETS!!

Before I continue describing the 6 and 8 play, there is one other fact that you should know. In one form or another, the 6 and 8 bets have BURIED (broke) more crapshooters than ALL THE OTHER BETS ON THE CRAP TABLE COMBINED!! This statement can be verified by any experienced (whether 30 or 60 years of age) Crap Game operator. (Don't ask him to put it in writing.) I should add that the 6 and 8 are by far THE MOST OFTEN PLAYED box numbers on the craps layout.

Whether or not I originated this particular play on the 6 and 8, I'll never know. After experimenting I came up with the different moves, including the STOP LOSSES outlined in this play.

I can honestly say that I have been quite pleased with the BATTING AVERAGE of THIS play.

Now that I have reassured you as to the MERIT of the SECOND LEAST WORST BET, let me show you how to suffer a little less severely when making this play.

(1) Your first move is deciding on the size of your Betting Stake. For example: You are a $5 plus odds Pass Line Bettor. To the Pass Line Bet, you would add the most that you could take in SINGLE ODDS. This would be $6 in odds behind the 5 or the 9, making the TOTAL bet $11. Add to this $11, another $12 each on the 6 and/or 8 for a total of $35, that we could (barring crap rolls) invest on any one QUALIFIED SHOOTER. (We at all times adhere to our BASIC STRATEGY BETTING RULES, which tells us who qualifies as a QUALIFIED SHOOTER.) We multiply this $35 by 10 for a Total Betting Stake of $350.

Should the 6 or 8 become the Pass Line Point, you would still bet $12 on the opposite number. Should you make the Pass Line Point of a 6 or 8 and then come out on a point other than the 6 or 8, you would fill in the open box with $12. Regardless of how large the opposite number may have grown, you still fill the open box with the minimum amount. (In our case $12.) You never take money from a winning number and add to a non-winning number. This is a bad habit of far too many Place and Buy Bet Bettors.

By betting $12 each on the 6 or 8, and 10 or $11 on a completed Pass Line plus Odds Bet, we are keeping ALL THREE BETS (the 6 and 8, and the Pass Line plus odds bet) as close to being AS EQUAL IN SIZE AS POSSIBLE. (To start with.) This way, we eliminate any GUESSING as to which of the three numbers will do the most for us. The $25 plus odds Pass Line Bettor, would Place Bet the 6 and 8 for $60 each. (You can work out the size of your own bets accordingly.)

At all times keep in mind YOUR TOTAL GAMBLING BANKROLL. As an occasional player, you should not use more than 5% for any ONE betting Stake, which in turn will cover 10 QUALIFIED SHOOTERS.

(2) We place our Betting Stake of $350 in the FRONT or BETTING PORTION of the chip rack.

(3) We wait for a Qualified Shooter and then make a $5 bet on the Pass Line. The shooter rolls a 4 and we take $5 in odds.

(4) We Place Bet the 6 and 8 for $12 each.

(5) The shooter rolls an 8 and we win $14. We increase our $12 Place Bet on the 8 to $18. We place the remaining $8 into the REAR or LOCK-UP PORTION of the chip rack. The shooter again rolls an 8 and we win $21. We increase the $18 Place Bet on the 8 to $30, place the remaining $9 into the lock-up rack. The shooter rolls a third 8 and we win $35. We increase our $30 Place Bet on the 8 to $42, and the remaining $23 is placed into the lock-up rack. The shooter rolls the Pass Line Point of 4, and we receive a total payoff of $25.

(6) We now increase our Pass Line Bet to $7. The shooter rolls an 8, and we take $10 in odds. This leaves us with a balance of $8 from the $25 we received when the Pass

Line Point of 4 was made. The $8 is placed into the lock-up rack. At the same time we take down (have the dealer return to us) the $42 that we had Place Bet on the 8. This $42 is also placed into the lock-up rack. Had we not shown a profit on the $12 that we originally bet on the 8, we would have returned it to the FRONT or BETTING STAKE PORTION of the chip rack . . . NOT the lock-up rack!! . . . (No profit . . . No lock-up.)

We leave the $12 Place Bet on the 6 as is. (The $12 Place Bet on the 6 hasn't made us a dime, so don't take any money from the 8 and add it to the 6. This is a bad habit that many Place and Buy Bettors have.)

In the BASIC STRATEGY PLAY FOR THE RIGHT BETTOR, I recommended an approximate 50% INCREASE in your winning Pass Line Bets. You also increase your winning Place Bets by the same approximate 50%. What I am attempting to do is show you the most painless way of living with these HIGH FATALITY RATE BETS. Who knows? You might possibly, (but I'm afraid temporarily) outlive the Basic Strategy Player. The extra investment, plus the numerous winning bets required just to break even on any one shooter, will show you THE HIGH FATALITY RATE you are facing.

(7) The shooter makes his Pass Line Point of 8 and we receive a total payoff of $36. We now increase our Pass Line Bet to $10. The shooter rolls a Natural (7 or 11). We now have $20 on the Pass Line. We PARLAY (or let ride) the $20. The shooter rolls a 9. We do NOT take any odds behind our Pass Line Bet. (You will recall, in our Basic Strategy Play for the Right Bettor, that I called taking advantage of Naturals (7 or 11) the smartest bet on the crap table. The reasons being, that we get 3 to 1 on a COMPLETED PARLAY. At the same time we SALVAGE or DO NOT USE the odds portion that had been EARMARKED FOR THIS BET.)

We Place Bet $12 in the hole left open on the 8. We leave the $12 Place Bet on the 6 as is. In making the Pass Line Point of 8, we received $36. Of this $36, we used $10 on our Pass Line Bet, plus $12 that we filled in on the EMPTY BOX for the Place Bet 8. We are left with $14 that we place into the lock-up rack. The shooter makes his Pass Line Point of 9 and our parlay is COMPLETED. We receive a TOTAL payoff of $40 for our original $10.

Regardless of the amount that we take down from the 6 or 8 when it becomes the Pass Line Point, should we make the point (6 or 8) and then come out on a point other than the 6 or 8, we would replace the open box 6 or 8 with our MINIMUM BET. (In our case $12.) This is one of our STOP LOSS MOVES to keep the seven-out or miss-out laydown on the crap table as small as possible. Our other STOP LOSS is the CRAP ROLL on the COME-OUT ROLL for a new Pass Line Point. At this time we start over again on the Pass Line with our MINIMUM BET plus odds. At the same time, should we have any increases in the size of our 6 and 8 Place Bets, we would also reduce these to their MINIMUM SIZE PLACE BETS. (In our case $12 each.) Got that straight??

(8) We increase our Pass Line Bet to $15. The shooter comes out on a Crap Roll and we lose our $15 bet. We now return to our MINIMUM BET of $5 on the PASS LINE. The shooter rolls a 10 and we take $5 in odds. This leaves us with a balance of $15 from the $40 that we received on our Completed Parlay. We place this $15 into the lock-up rack. The $12 Place Bets on the 6 and 8 are left as is. The shooter sevens out and the Hand or Shoot is over. We must now wait for our next Qualified Shooter before we make our next bet.

(9) On the last remaining bet in our Betting Stake, we may if necessary, take

enough chips from our lock-up rack to properly finish that ONE bet.

(10) When we have used up our Betting Stake, we count the lock-up chips. Should we find that we have enough chips in total (not just winnings) to move up to OUR NEXT HIGHER LEVEL, we do so and cash in or pocket the balance. Our next higher Betting Stake would now be $510. This would allow us to start out by betting $7 plus SINGLE ODDS on the Pass Line. Our 6 and 8 Place Bets would now start at $18 each.

Should we find that we have made a profit of ANY amount, but not enough to move to our next higher level, we would STILL remain at the same table. We pocket or cash in any profit, and start over again with the same $350.

Should you on the other hand, show a loss (bite your tongue) on our CURRENT BETTING STAKE, move on to the next consecutively numbered table, and start over again with whatever your TOTAL GAMBLING BANKROLL now permits. (Always let your Total Gambling Bankroll tell you the size of the Betting Stake to use.) It is for this reason, that the professional gambler VERY SELDOM if ever goes broke. Never be embarrassed to reduce the size of your Betting Stake when the dice are going against you. I've said it many times before, but it still bears repeating: DIMES WILL BECOME DOLLARS, IF AND WHEN THE DICE SHOULD TURN FOR YOU . . . Providing you are PLAYING FOR KEEPS . . .

INCREASE YOUR WINNING PASS LINE PLUS ODDS BETS . . . AS FOLLOWS:
5-7-10-15-25-35-50-75-125-175-250-350-500-700-1000-1500-2500-3000-etc.

INCREASE YOUR WINNING 6 or 8 PLACE BETS . . . AS FOLLOWS:
12-18-30-42-60-90-120-180-300-420-600-900-1200-1800-3000-etc.

THE INSIDE NUMBERS (5-6-8-9) PLAY FOR THE RIGHT BETTOR

Second only to the 6 and 8 PLAY, the INSIDE NUMBERS (5-6-8-9) PLAY is the most popular numbers play. This play and a couple of others are for the DREAMERS who believe that every shooter picking up the dice, will roll at least 20 or 30 PAYOFF NUMBERS. (Keep dreaming children!! Perhaps all of your dreams won't wind up becoming NIGHTMARES.)

(1) As is usual, our first move is deciding on THE SIZE OF YOUR TOTAL BETTING STAKE. As a $5 plus odds Pass Line Bettor, (barring crap rolls) the most that we could invest on any one shooter would be $54. This $54 would allow us to bet $5 on the Pass Line plus SINGLE ODDS, plus $10 each on the 5 and 9, and $12 each on the 6 and 8.

Since in ALL of our plays for the Right Bettor, we allow for enough in our Betting Stake to cover approximately 10 QUALIFIED SHOOTERS, we would require a TOTAL BETTING STAKE of $540.

(2) We place the Betting Stake in the FRONT or BETTING PORTION of the CHECK RACK, and wait for a Qualified Shooter before we make our first bet on the Pass Line.

(3) We bet $5 on the Pass Line and the shooter rolls a 4. We take $5 in odds. We Place Bet $10 each on the 5 and 9, and $12 each on the 6 and 8. The shooter rolls a 5 and we receive $14 in winnings. (Our $10 Place Bet on the 5 is still up.) We increase our $10 Place Bet on the 5 to $15, and place the remaining $9 in the REAR or LOCK-UP PORTION of the CHECK RACK. The shooter rolls a 6 and we win $14. We increase the $12 Place Bet on the 6 to $18, and place the remaining $8 into the lock-up rack. The shooter rolls a 9, and we win $14. We increase the $10 Place Bet on the 9 to $15, and the remaining $9 is placed into the lock-up rack. The shooter rolls the Pass Line Point of 4, and we receive a TOTAL PAYOFF of $25.

(4) We now INCREASE our Pass Line Bet to $7. The shooter rolls a 5 for the Pass Line Point. We take $8 in odds. This makes a total of $15 we have used of the $25 we received on making the Pass Line Point of 4. We place the remaining $10 into the lock-up rack. We also TAKE DOWN, (have the dealer return to us) the $15 we had Place Bet on the 5, and place it into the lock-up rack. ALL OTHER BETS are left as they are.

(5) The shooter makes his Pass Line Point of 5, and we receive a total payoff of $34. We now make an increased Pass Line Bet of $10, and the shooter rolls a NATURAL (7 or 11). We now have $20 on the Pass Line. We PARLAY (or let ride) the entire $20. The shooter rolls a 6. We DO NOT TAKE ANY ODDS. We have the dealer TAKE DOWN and return to us the $18 Place Bet we had going on the 6. We place this $18 into the lock-up rack.

Again, I will remind you of what I believe to be THE SMARTEST BET ON THE CRAP TABLE FOR THE RIGHT BETTOR. That is to PARLAY either TWO consecutive Naturals (7 or 11), or ONE Natural and ONE Pass Line Point, on which we do NOT take the odds. In so doing, we are SALVAGING THE ODDS that we had earmarked for this bet, and STILL have a 3 to 1 bet going for us.

We now make a $10 Place Bet on the open box 5. This make $20 we have used of the $34 we received when the shooter made his Pass Line Point of 5. This leaves us with a balance of $14, that we place into the lock-up rack. The shooter makes his Pass Line Point of 6, and we receive $40. OUR PARLAY IS COMPLETED.

(6) We now make an increased Pass Line Bet of $15. The shooter comes out on a CRAP ROLL, and we lose the $15 bet. We now BACK DOWN (or return) to our MINIMUM Pass Line Bet of $5. The shooter rolls a 10, and we take $5 in odds. We make a $12 Place bet on the open box 6. This makes a total of $37 that we used of the $40 we received on our completed parlay. We place the remaining $3 into the lock-up rack. Since the CRAP ROLL on our come-out roll for a new Pass Line Point is one of our STOP LOSS moves, we take down (have the dealer return to us) ANY INCREASES in our Place Bets, which we place into our lock-up rack. Our INSIDE NUMBERS are now back to their original minimum bets. ($10 each on the 5 and 9, and $12 each on the 6 and 8.)

I can't emphasize strongly enough, the importance of adhering to the STOP LOSS BETTING RULES. These stop loss moves, (if and when they show) is your best chance of overcoming the WEAKNESS of MULTI-NUMBER BETS.

I'll repeat again: These stop losses are the CRAP ROLL on the COME-OUT ROLL FOR A NEW PASS LINE POINT, that calls for us to REDUCE ALL BETS to their ORIGINAL MINIMUM SIZE. The other stop loss is when a BOX POINT (5-6-8-9) becomes THE PASS LINE POINT. ALL the money from that box number is placed into the LOCK-UP RACK. Should we later replace a bet on an EMPTY BOX, it is always with the ORIGINAL MINIMUM BET. It's a pretty nice feeling, when you see a well built up box number become the PASS LINE POINT. You can now take down and lock up the entire amount, knowing that should you have to replace a bet in the same box, it would only be with the minimum bet. (In our case, $10 or $12.)

(7) On the VERY LAST BET in our Betting Stake, we may if necessary, take enough from our lock-up rack to properly complete that ONE LAST BET.

(8) When we have used up the entire Betting Stake, we count our lock-up chips. Should we have enough to move up to our NEXT HIGHER LEVEL, we do so and pocket or cash in the balance. (Our next higher betting level is $7 plus odds on the Pass Line . . to begin with. Our next higher Place Bets are $15 each on the 5 and 9, and $18 each on the 6 and 8.) This comes to a TOTAL of $80 that we could (barring crap rolls) invest on any one shooter. You multiply this $80 by 10 for a TOTAL BETTING STAKE of $800. You do the same with whatever size betting stake YOU might care to use.

Should we show a win of ANY AMOUNT over our Original $540 Betting Stake, but less than our next HIGHER Betting Stake ($800), we STILL remain at the same table and start again with our $540 Betting Stake. We pocket or cash in any winnings. No matter how small, YOU NEVER QUIT A WINNING TABLE!!

Should we show a LOSS on our $540 Betting Stake, we would move on to the next CONSECUTIVELY NUMBERED table, and start again with our MINIMUM BETTING STAKE. (At all times, keep a record of your TOTAL GAMBLING BANKROLL and bet accordingly. The occasional gambler 5%. The regular gambler 1 or 2%.)

WE INCREASE OUR WINNING PASS LINE BETS AS FOLLOWS:
5-7-10-15-25-35-50-75-125-175-250-350-500-700-1000-1500-2500-etc.

WE INCREASE OUR WINNING PLACE BETS AS FOLLOWS:
(5 and 9) 10-15-25-35-50-75-125-175-250-350-500-700-1000-1500-2500-etc.
(6 and 8) 12-18-30-42-60-90-120-180-300-420-600-900-1200-1800-3000-etc.

THE OUTSIDE NUMBERS (4-5-9-10) PLAY

The OUTSIDE NUMBERS PLAY (4-5-9-10), is the same as the INSIDE NUMBERS PLAY, except that we replace th 6 and 8 with the 4 and 10. In this play we pay the 5% COMMISSION and BUY BET the 4 and 10. We save approximately 1.3/4% over Place Betting the 4 and 10. We DO however Place Bet the 5 and 9.

(1) As a $5 plus Odds Pass Line Bettor, we would (barring crap rolls) require $51 for any one QUALIFIED SHOOTER. Multiply this $51 by 10 for a TOTAL BETTING STAKE of $510.

Should one of the Outside Numbers (4-5-9-10) become the Pass Line Point, we would not require the full $51 for that particular shooter. Naturals OR Crap Rolls on the Come-Out Roll for a new Pass Line Point, would also affect the number of Qualified Shooters that you would be able to cover with your Betting Stake. We place our Betting Stake into the FRONT or BETTING PORTION of the CHIP RACK, and wait for a Qualified Shooter before we make our first pass line bet.

(2) We bet $5 on the Pass Line and the shooter rolls a 6. We take $5 in Odds.

(3) We Place Bet the 5 and 9 for $10 each. We BUY BET the 4 and 10 for $10 each. By paying the dealer the 5% commission on the 4 and 10, we get 2 to 1 instead of 9 to 5 that we would get by PLACE BETTING them. (You should always take advantage of this option.)

(4) The shooter rolls a 5, and we win $14. We increase our $10 Place Bet on the 5 to $15, and place the remaining $9 into the lock-up rack. The shooter rolls a 10, and we win $20. We PRESS (or double) our $10 Buy Bet on the 10 to $20. In Buy Betting the 10 for $20, we give the dealer $1 in commission and the remaining $9 is placed into the lock-up rack. Where we increase winning bets on the 5-6-8-9 by approximately 50%, on the 4 and 10, we pay the 5% commission and increase any winning bets by 100%. This still leaves us with more than 40% for our lock-up rack. The shooter again rolls a 10 and we win $40. We give the dealer $22 and increase our $20 Buy Bet on the 10 to $40. We lock up the remaining $18. The shooter rolls a 5, and we increase our $15 Place Bet on the 5 to $25. The remaining $11 is placed into the lock-up rack. There will be times when the SAME number will repeat itself in bunches. This is the best thing that could happen to the Place or Buy Bettor.

Before I continue with the Outside Numbers Play, I would like to explain A VERY POPULAR PLAY ON THE 4 and 10. Normally, when Buy Betting the 4 or 10 for $10, should it be rolled, you would win $20. By paying the 5% commission, you would again have a $10 Buy Bet working on whichever number was rolled. However, in OUR play, we PRESS (or double) our bet to $20. After paying the 5% or $1 commission, we still have $9, or more than 40% for our LOCK-UP.

On the other hand, and although it would cut down on your INITIAL winning lock-up, I would recommend increasing your Buy Bet on the 4 or 10 to $25 instead of $20. (With the exception of the odd Mickey Mouse joint, most casinos will let you Buy Bet the $25 bet for the same $1 that they charge you for the $20 Buy Bet.) In so doing, you would increase your winning bets on the 4 or 10 as follows: 10-25-50-100-etc. On reaching the $100 bet, the House would charge you the straight 5%.

What we are giving up in increasing our FIRST winning bet to $25 instead of $20, is $5 less for your initial lock-up. ($4 instead of $9.) It's your money and your choice on how you would like to play the 4 and 10 bet. The main reason I have of approving of this change in play, is that since these multi-number plays are anyways "LONGSHOT LOUEY PLAYS", then go all the way as a LONGSHOT PLAYER. Who knows? It could in a NO BRAINER hand or shoot, pay for itself MANY TIMES OVER!!

I don't QUITE put the Inside Numbers, the Outside Numbers, or the Across the Boards plays into the same category as the IDIOT or CHRISTMAS TREE plays, but you must admit that they are close to being KISSIN KUZZINS. The 6 and 8 play?? It is not exactly an ILLEGITIMATE MEMBER of the SAME FAMILY EITHER!!

While we've been discussing these 4 and 10 plays, the shooter has been busy rolling lots of numbers. (It should only happen.) We have increased our 5 and 9 to $50, and the 4 and 10 to $100 each. To top it off, the shooter just made our Pass Line Point of 6. We receive a total payoff of $21. (Ain't it wonderful how easy it is, when we make mind bets?? Unfortunately, I have as yet to find a dice joint that will BOOK MY MIND BETS!!)

(5) We now increase our Pass Line Bet to $7. The shooter rolls a 4, and we take $7 in

Odds. We place the remaining $7 into the lock-up rack. We also take down (have the dealer return to us) the $100 Buy Bet on the 4. This $100 plus the $5 we paid to Buy Bet the 4, is also placed into the lock-up rack. The remaining Place and Buy Bets are left as they are.

(6) The shooter makes his Pass Line Point of 4, and we receive a total payoff of $35. We make an increased Pass Line Bet of $10, and the shooter rolls a NATURAL (7 or 11). We now have $20 on the Pass Line. We PARLAY (or let ride) the $20. The shooter rolls a 5. We do NOT take the odds. We pay the dealer 50¢ for vig or commission and Buy Bet the 4 for $10. Should the House charge a minimum of $1 for ANY buy Bet, (let them stick it). We PLACE BET the 4 for $10. We place the remaining $14.50?? from our winning bet on the Pass Line Point of 4, into the lock-up rack.

(7) The shooter makes his Pass Line Point of 5, and we receive a total payoff of $40. OUR PARLAY IS NOW COMPLETE.

(8) We now make an increased Pass Line Bet of $15. The shooter comes out on a CRAP ROLL and we lose our $15 bet. We now back down to our Minimum Pass Line Bet of $5. The shooter rolls an 8 and we take $5 in odds. We Place Bet the empty box on the 5 for $10. This leaves us with a balance of $5 from the $40 we collected on our completed parlay. We place this $5 into the lock-up rack. Since the Crap Roll on the shooter's Come-out Roll for a NEW Pass Line Point is one of our STOP LOSS MOVES, we reduce any increased Place or Buy Bets to their MINIMUM bet of $10 each. Anything over is placed into the lock-up rack.

(9) The shooter sevens out, and the hand or shoot is finished. We now wait for a QUALIFIED SHOOTER before we make our next bet. On the LAST bet in our Betting Stake, we may if necessary, take enough from our lock-up chips to properly complete that ONE bet.

(10) When we have used our entire Betting Stake, we count the lock-up checks. Should we have enough to move up to our next higher Betting Level, we do so and pocket or cash in the balance. Our next HIGHER LEVEL would call for a Pass Line Bet of $7 plus Odds. Our Place Bets on the 5 and 9 would be $15 each. Our Buy Bets on the 4 and 10 would also be $15 each. The most we could invest on any one Qualified Shooter (barring crap rolls) would be $78.50. Multiply this by 10, for a TOTAL BETTING STAKE of $785.

Should we show a win of ANY AMOUNT over the $510, but less than $785, (our next higher betting level) we would REMAIN AT THE SAME TABLE and start over again with our original $510 Betting Stake. Should we show a LOSS on our $510 Betting Stake, we would move on to the next CONSECUTIVELY NUMBERED table and start over again with your MINIMUM BETTING STAKE.

P.S. Count your Total Gambling Bankroll at the end of a full day's play, not after EACH betting stake is played out. Be a crapshooter, not a bookkeeper!!

WE INCREASE OUR PASS LINE PLUS ODDS BET AS FOLLOWS
5-7-10-15-25-35-50-75-125-175-250-350-500-700-1000-1500-2500-etc.

WE INCREASE OUR WINNING PLACE BETS AS FOLLOWS
(5 and 9) 10-15-25-35-50-75-125-175-250-350-500-700-1000-1500-2500-etc.

WE INCREASE OUR WINNING BUY BETS AS FOLLOWS
(4 and 10) 10-25-50-100-200-400-800-1600-etc.
(or 4 and 10 this way) 10-20-40-80-160-320-640-1280-etc.

ACROSS THE BOARD (4-5-6-8-9-10) PLAY

Here is the ONE method of play that eliminates all the guesswork, as to which numbers to play. YOU PLAY ALL OF THEM.

Should this be your choice of plays, then just hope that if or when your ELIGIBLE SHOOTER rolls the dice 8 times, that he will roll the SAME NUMBER all 8 times. That's about how much chance you have of beating this 6 NUMBER PLAY.

I may be exaggerating slightly, but I assure you, very slightly. I won't say that I haven't seen some big scores made on this play, I have however, many more times seen BRICK WALL BILLIES.* (*Losers.)

The Betting Rules for the ACROSS THE BOARD PLAY is almost a repeat performance of the INSIDE NUMBERS and the OUTSIDE NUMBERS PLAYS. In both the Inside or Outside Numbers Play, you would have either 4 or 5 numbers in play. In the Across-the-board Play, you have ALL 6 numbers in play at ALL times. I recommend the Across-the-board Play OVER the Inside or Outside Numbers Play.

There is nothing as exasperating for the multi-number player, than having one or two empty boxes, and then have those one or two numbers rolled again and again, while your other 4 or 5 numbers remain virgin. (Or at best, just slightly pregnant.)

In the Basic Strategy Betting Rules for the Right Bettor, the dice did all the handicapping (or number selection) for us. ALL WE had to do was to make our bets on the PASS LINE. The rolls of the dice told us when to INCREASE our bets. When to PARLAY our bets. When to BACK DOWN. Together with sensible MONEY MANAGEMENT, these moves are all there is to the PROPER PLAY of Craps, as well as the proper operation of your BUSINESS or PROFESSIONAL life.

When we buy or place bet SPECIFIC numbers, we are strictly GUESSING. In this play we are using ALL 6 numbers. We have at least eliminated the guess work. Value-wise this is an IDIOT PLAY. However, properly played it at least has the merit of an INTELLIGENT IDIOT PLAY.

(1) You arrive at the size of your Total Betting Stake in the following manner: A $5 plus odds Pass Line Bettor would, (barring crap rolls) require a maximum of $11, plus $54 across the board on the remaining 5 numbers, plus $1.00 vigorish or commission for BUY BETTING the 4 and 10. This comes to a total of $66 you could invest (or risk) on any one shooter. You multiply this $66 by 10 for a TOTAL BETTING STAKE of $660. This $660 allows you enough to bet on approximately 10 QUALIFIED SHOOTERS. You place your Betting Stake into the FRONT or BETTING PORTION of the CHECK RACK. The $25 plus odds Pass Line Bettor would require a Betting Stake of $3300. You can figure out your own betting stake by using the $5 bettor's formula.

(2) We wait for a QUALIFIED SHOOTER, and then bet $5 on the Pass Line. The shooter rolls a 6 and we take $5 in odds.

(3) We Place Bet the 5 and 9 for $10 each. We Place Bet the 8 for $12. By giving the dealer an extra 5%, or as in our case $1, we BUY BET the 4 and 10 for $10 each. By BUY BETTING the 4 and 10, we get 2 to 1 instead of 9 to 5 on any winning bets. (It is therefore to your advantage to BUY BET the 4 and 10. It is to your advantage to PLACE BET the 5-6-8-9.)

(4) The shooter rolls a 5, and we receive $14 in winnings. We increase our $10 Place Bet on the 5 to $15. The remaining $9 is placed into the lock-up rack. The shooter rolls a 10 and we receive $20 in winnings. We PRESS (or double) our $10 Buy Bet to $20.

The dealer deducts the $1 commission on the $20 Buy Bet and we place the remaining $9 into the lock-up rack.

(Again I'll repeat.) We increase our winning PLACE BETS on the 5-6-8-9 by approximately 50%. (The increases alternately varies between 40 some odd percent, and 70 some odd percent. Leaving us with a lock-up that also varies about the same percent.) The figures are approximate, so I don't need some smart ass COMPUTER CRAPSHOOTERS catching me in a mathematical mistake. I've made more mistakes at the crap table than I've had hair on my head. I've paid thru the lungs for every one of them!!

On the 4 and 10, we increase our winning BUY BETS by 100%. (Or more simply put, we DOUBLE our BUY BETS on every winning roll.) After paying the 5% vig or commission, we still lock up more than 40% on each winning roll.

The shooter rolls another 10, and we receive $40. We press (or double) our $20 Buy Bet on the 10 to $40. After paying the $2 commission, we place the remaining $18 into the lock-up rack. I've said it before and I'll say it again. When you Place or Buy numbers, don't be disappointed when one of the numbers keeps repeating itself, while the other numbers remain untouched.

It is a BIG ADVANTAGE to have the SAME number rolled repeatedly, rather than bits and pieces spread all over the layout. (This is the classic example of where the "ONE GOOD ONE" makes up for blah . . . blah . . . blah".)

(5) After rolling a few more numbers, the shooter makes his Pass Line Point of 6. We receive a total payoff of $21.

(6) We now make an INCREASED Pass Line Bet of $7, and the shooter comes out on a 10. We take $7 in odds and place the remaining $7 into the lock-up rack. We also have the dealer TAKE DOWN (return to us) the entire $40 Buy Bet that we have on the 10. The dealer also returns the $2 commission that we paid in Buy Betting the 10. From this $42, we Place Bet the 6 for $12, and the remaining $30 is placed into the lock-up rack. All other Place and Buy Bets are left as they are.

(7) The shooter makes his Pass Line Point of 10, and we receive a total payoff of $35. We now make an increased Pass Line Bet of $10. The shooter rolls a NATURAL (7 or 11). This gives us a total of $20 on the Pass Line. We PARLAY (or let ride) the entire $20, and the shooter rolls an 8. We do NOT take any odds as we have a parlay started. Win or lose, the start of a parlay means that we have at least salvaged the odds portion, which had been earmarked for this bet. The shooter makes his Pass Line Point of 8, and we receive a total of $40. Our parlay is COMPLETE.

(8) We make a $15 bet on the Pass Line. The shooter comes out on a Crap Roll. We lose the $15 bet and now back down to our minimum bet of $5 on the Pass Line. The shooter rolls a 6 and we take $5 in odds. We Place Bet the empty box on the 8 for $12. This leaves us with a balance of $3 from the $40 we received on our completed parlay. We place this $3 into the lock-up rack. Also, as we do when a Crap-Roll shows on the Come-out Roll for a new PASS LINE POINT, we reduce ALL our Place and Buy Bets to their MINIMUM and whatever remains is placed into the lock-up rack.

(9) The shooter sevens out, and the Hand or shoot is over. We must now wait for our next Qualified Shooter. Again I'll repeat, that on our LAST and ONLY on our last Qualified Shooter, we may if necessary, take enough from our lock-up rack to properly complete the bet.

(10) After your last bet, you count the lock-up checks. Should you have enough in

your TOTAL COUNT (not just the winnings) to move up to your NEXT HIGHER LEVEL in your Betting Stake AND your initial increased Pass Line Bet, we do so and pocket or cash in the balance. Regardless of the amount of our winnings, we NEVER move up more than one level at a time. (Let the House TAKE THE STEAM and chase THEIR losses.) Your next higher Betting Stake is $975.

Should we show any profit on our Betting Stake, we would still remain at the SAME table and start over again with the SAME Betting Stake of $660. Should we show a LOSS on our Betting Stake, we would move on to the next consecutively numbered table, and start over again with our $660 (or whatever yours is) MINIMUM Betting Stake.

FOLLOWING ARE THE WINNING INCREASES THAT YOU USE IN THIS PLAY

Pass Line Plus Odds:-5-7-10-15-25-35-50-75-125-250-350-500-700-1000-etc.
5 and 9 PLACE BETS:-10-15-25-35-50-75-125-175-250-350-500-700-1000-etc.
6 and 8 PLACE BETS:-12-18-30-42-60-90-120-180-300-420-600-900-1200-etc.
4 and 10 BUY BETS:-10-20-40-80-160-320-640-1280-etc.
Or 4 and 10 BUY BETS:-10-25-50-100-200-400-800-1600-etc.

Should your gambling bankroll be in the 25¢ Crap Table category, or should you wish to experiment with smaller betting units, then use the following:
Pass Line Bets, Plus odds:-75¢-1.25-1.75-2.50-3.50-5.00-etc.
5 and 9 Place Bets:-2.50-3.75-5.00-7.50-10.00-etc.
6 and 8 Place Bets:-3.00-4.50-6.00-9.00-12.00-etc.
4 and 10 Place and Buy Bets:-Place Bet-2.50--Buy Bet-5.00-10.00-etc.

MULTIPLE ODDS BET FOR THE RIGHT BETTOR

Prior to 1980, all Bank Crap games (legal casino or illegal floating crap games) dealt either SINGLE or DOUBLE ODDS.

It was in 1980 that BOB STUPAK'S VEGAS WORLD on the Strip in Las Vegas started dealing TRIPLE ODDS. In Atlantic City, where until 1983 all casinos were dealing DOUBLE ODDS, two casinos (THE GOLDEN NUGGET and RESORTS INTERNATIONAL) started dealing TRIPLE ODDS. At the same time, the VEGAS CLUB and the BARBARY COAST in Las Vegas, also started dealing TRIPLE ODDS.

However, prior to this in December of 1982, BENNY BINION'S HORSESHOE

CASINO in Las Vegas, started dealing QUINTUPLE ODDS, and just one month later in January of 1983, they topped this and went to dealing 10 TIMES ODDS. (As of today, they are still dealing 10 times odds.)

Any crapshooter can come in off the street and make a minimum bet of 50¢ on the Pass or the Don't Pass Line. Or if he wishes he can bet as much as $1,000 on the Pass or the Don't Pass Line, and then take $10,000 in odds, or if betting Wrong, lay enough to win up to $10,000 behind the Pass-line Point.

Should you want to bet higher than the "off the street limits" then they will accommodate you. Just ask for one of the Binions, (Sons, Jack or Teddy, or Benny the father himself.) Should none of the Binions be around, then whoever is in charge at that time of day or night, will arrange for any limits you wish. Understandably, your "off the shoulder" or starting bets would have to be higher than "off the street" bets for the established limits.

I had many years earlier proven to myself that Multiple Odds were a definite advantage for the Wrong Bettor, providing he used certain "STOP LOSS MOVES."

The Right Bettor, on the other hand is at a disadvantage in taking Multiple Odds behind his Pass-line Bet. Mathematically, it DOES cut down on the House Percentage against him. However, at the crap table it's a different story. Once a Pass-line point is established, the Right Bettor must accept the fact that he is the UNDERDOG, as opposed to the Wrong Bettor who (win or lose) is a FAVORITE TO WIN HIS BET.

In 1980 I began experimenting in "live" action with TRIPLE ODDS" for the Right Bettor. After literally thousands of hands or shoots in "money action" I found the following method of play to show a winning Batting Average, that comes quite close to the batting average of my Basic Strategy method of play. (Between 60% and 70%. Which means that for every 10 Betting Stakes that I issue, 6 or 7 of them show a net profit of a little or a lot.) Due also to my Money Management moves, I have never as yet run into a complete loss of my Betting Stake. My smallest losses have been under 10% of a Betting Stake. My biggest losses have been almost 80% of any single Betting Stake. My wins have also been as little as under 10%, while at other times, they have been as big as MANY times the size of my Betting Stake.

It is the limiting of losses, but NEVER limiting the size of your wins, that I feel is the smartest move any gambler (or businessman) can make.

The limited few TRULY PROFESSIONAL gamblers I've known in my lifetime have also had another "STOP LOSS MOVE" going for them. They were never embarrassed to back down on the size of their Betting Stakes when the dice or the cards were going against them. I for one, try not to forget my own quote: "DIMES WILL BECOME DOLLARS, IF AND WHEN THE DICE SHOULD TURN FOR ME."

The Pass-line portion of your bet will be approximately one half of the entire bet, earmarked for any one QUALIFIED SHOOTER. (In case you haven't read either my book "THE DICE DOCTOR" or VOLUME #6 of CASINO and SPORTS, in order to become a qualified shooter, the shooter must either roll a Natural (7 or 11) on his Come-out Roll, or else establish a Pass-line Point (4-5-6-8-9-10) and then make the point.

Starting with a $15 plus SINGLE ODDS Pass-line bet, together with two $5 Come Bets with TRIPLE ODDS, you would require a Betting Stake of $860. Your two Come Bets will remain at $5 plus Triple Odds throughout your $860 and $1010 Betting Stakes. On your 3rd and 4th Betting Stake level of $1650 and $1800, your two Come

Bets will now be $10 plus TRIPLE ODDS. After I have described this play in detail, I will show the approximate 50% increase in the size of your winning Pass-line plus maximum SINGLE ODDS bets. At the same time, I will list the size of each Come Bet with TRIPLE ODDS required, depending on the size of your Betting Stake.

The Total Betting Stake will allow enough for bets on approximately 10 QUALIFIED SHOOTERS. The Betting Stake is placed in the FRONT portion of the chip rack. After you have had a winning Pass-line bet and then completed your following increased bet, whatever remains is placed into the REAR or LOCK-UP portion of your chip rack. O.K. children. Let's shoot craps!!

(1) We wait for a QUALIFIED SHOOTER and then make a $15 bet on the Pass-line. Should the shooter roll a Craps, (1-1, 1-2, 6-6) we again make a $15 bet on the Pass Line. Once a player becomes a Qualified Shooter, we continue making these $15 Pass-line bets until a point (4-5-6-8-9-10) is established, at which time we take SINGLE ODDS. Should the shooter roll a Natural (7 or 11) we PARLAY or let ride the entire amount. (In our case, $30.) Should the shooter roll a second consecutive Natural, our Parlay would now be completed, for a total of $60 for our original $15 bet. Our next bet would be $25 on the Pass Line. On the other hand, should the shooter have rolled a pass-line point with the $30 (or started parlay) we would NOT take any odds. In getting a Parlay started, (unless the shooter rolls a Craps on his second roll, after rolling a Natural on his first roll) we are at the very least salvaging the Odds portion that we had earmarked for this bet, and still have a 4 for 1, or $60 for $15 bet going for us.

(2) Our next move is to bet $5 on the Come Line. We follow the same moves we had on the Pass Line bet, except that we take TRIPLE ODDS when we have established a point.

(3) We would now try for a second Come Bet with Triple Odds. Should we win a Come Bet, we would continue making and keeping two Come Bets in action at all times. What we are trying to do is to grind out extra money on these Come Bets, while our larger main bets are on the Pass Line. There will be times when we win numerous Come Bets and not have too much luck with our Pass Line bet. As crapshooters, we know and accept that anything can and does happen at the crap table. Don't ever be surprised if the so-called Law of Averages goes LOPSIDE LOUEY at times. The abnormal is quite often the normal, when it comes to shooting craps.

One other move to keep in mind when making Come Bets. Should we have a bet on the Come Line and the shooter rolls an Eleven (11), we would PARLAY or let it all ride. Should he then roll a point, we would only take DOUBLE ODDS instead of TRIPLE ODDS. Should the shooter roll two (2) consecutive Elevens, then we would Parlay it all and take SINGLE ODDS if his next roll is a point. Should a miracle take place and the shooter rolls three (3) consecutive Elevens, then you would take down your entire Parlay and start over again with a SINGLE UNIT. (In our case $5.)

Since on the Come Line, there's no chance of a Parlay starting with a Seven (7), then we should take full advantage of any Elevens that might show.

(4) Should we run into a streak of one or more consecutive Pass-line wins, and then have the shooter roll a Craps on his Come-out Roll for a new Pass-line point, we would return or back down to our original minimum Pass-line Bet. (In our case it would be $15 plus Single Odds.)

(5) On the very last bet remaining in our Betting Stake, we may if necessary take enough from our Lock-up Chips to properly complete that ONE LAST BET.

PASS LINE BET +	MAXIMUM SINGLE ODDS.	COME LINE +	TRIPLE ODDS.	TOTAL BETTING STAKE
$15	$25	$5	$18	$860
$25	$30	$5	$18	$1010
$35	$50	$10	$30	$1650
$50	$50	$10	$30	$1800
$75	$125	$20	$60	$3600
$125	$150	$20	$60	$4350
$175	$250	$40	$120	$7450
$250	$250	$40	$120	$8200
$350	$500	$80	$240	$14900
$500	$600	$80	$240	$17400

THE SILENT MINORITY
(THE WRONG BETTOR)

To the SILENT MINORITY at the crap table . . . the Wrong or Backline Bettor . . . a word or two . . . or three or four.

A a WRONG BETTOR, be prepared to be stared at, glared at, despised, scorned and cursed at. (Vocally as well as silently.) Not only by your fellow crapshooters, but to some extent even by the dealers. A very small percentage of Wrong Bettors, in comparison to the Right Bettors, will TOKE or MAKE BETS for the dealers.

A SMALL GEORGE (small tipper) among Wrong Bettors is ten times as scarce as a REAL or SUPER GEORGE (good to best tipper) is among the Right Bettors.

To one degree or another (acceptable or not) ALL GAMBLERS are superstitious and envious. The Wrong Bettors however are SO paranoid and sadistic, that they actually wish EACH OTHER bad luck!! This is in comparison to a table full of Right Bettors, who in a matter of minutes, can become bosom buddies, when a Hand or Shoot is rolled.

The Right Bettor can hoot and holler after every roll of the dice. Just let the Wrong Bettor call OUT LOUD for a miss-out seven, and he comes very close to taking his life in his hands.

Instead of hooting and hollering, the Wrong Bettor substitutes it with a seemingly religious alternative. Just watch the facial expressions and lip movements of MOST Wrong Bettors. Are you going to tell me that members of this MINORITY aren't in the midst of a CONTINUOUS SILENT PRAYER??

The average Wrong Bettor is on edge from the moment he makes his first bet, and win or lose, it doesn't end even when he is through at the crap table.

The pressure under which the Wrong Bettor puts himself, can best be likened to the STOCK MARKET BOOKIE that is always SELLING SHORT. Unlike the horse or sports book, the Wrong Bettor has NO WAY in which to BALANCE HIS BOOKS. (Except gutless hedging.)

In contrast to DALE CARNEGIE'S goal, you as a Wrong Bettor are not at the Crap Table to "WIN FRIENDS and INFLUENCE PEOPLE". I have as yet to hear a Wrong Bettor say, "HE IS PLAYING FOR FUN". You are there for one reason only. "TO WIN THE MONEY."

In following articles, I will give you enough tested and proven rules that may help you become a successful Wrong Bettor. . .
READ THEM . . . STUDY THEM . . . REMEMBER THEM . . . THEN GO OUT AND GET THE MONEY!!

7 YOU WIN . . . 7 YOU WIN

Everybody HATES the Wrong Bettor!! Even a fellow Wrong Bettor.

Here is one play by the Wrong Bettor that NOBODY hates. In this play, BOTH the Right and the Wrong Bettor is rooting for the 7 on the Come-out Roll. It is one of the many Road or Expense Money Plays used by the grinding Wrong Bettor. This is the only Wrong Betting Play (I know of) that doesn't antagonize the Right Bettor.

Before the Come-out Roll for a Pass Line Point, the Wrong Bettor will LAY BET $51 to win $25 against the 4 or 10. (One OR the other only.) Most casinos will charge you the same $1 vigorish or commission, that they would charge you to LAY BET $40 to win $20. In the Bahamas or the odd Mickey Mouse joint elsewhere, they will charge you $1.25. (Most casinos will also allow you to LAY BET $102 to win $50.) In betting $200 to win $100, or multiples of this amount, they will charge you the straight 5%.

Here's a BIG BONUS for those of you that are interested in making this bet in Las Vegas. BENNY BINION'S HORSESHOE CASINO in the downtown or GLITTER GULCH area, won't charge you anything unless you WIN your bet. This applies only to lay betting against the 4 or the 10. (The same deal goes for the Right Bettor that wants to BUY BET the 4 or 10.) The EL CORTEZ and THE VEGAS CLUB had also given this bonus for awhile, but as of the spring of 1984, they gave it up. However, casino operators are very unpredictable, so it's quite possible that they (or others) are running this deal again.

Taking the $51 to $25 bet as our example, these are the proper moves: You make your $51 LAY BET against the 4 or 10, (one or the other) BEFORE the shooter rolls the dice for a Pass Line Point. Should he roll a 7 on his Come-out Roll, you would be an INSTANT WINNER. By giving the dealer his $1 commission, you are paid up for the next Come-out Roll. What we are looking for, are a big bunch of consecutive 7's being rolled. (We've all seen it happen. RIGHT?? RIGHT!!)

Now, here USUALLY comes the second move. (One that makes nearly ALL crapshooters HATE the Wrong Bettor.) When a Pass Line Point is established, instead of his now taking down (having the dealer return to him) his $51 LAY BET, as this is PROPERLY played, this player will let the Lay Bet continue working against the shooter. He is now once again, the HATED Wrong Bettor.

This mathematical genius has trouble figuring out, that for every ONE lay bet he LOSES, he must WIN 3 lay bets in order to show a NET PROFIT. He could lose the same ONE bet out of three, by making it a ONE ROLL ONLY bet, but for some reason I haven't been able to answer, the percentage for a ONE ROLL BET doesn't average out to the same as an ALL DAY BET. Perhaps the following may be the answer: Bet the HARD EIGHT as an ALL DAY BET and you will be paid 9 to 1 if you win your bet. Now, bet that the shooter will make the hard eight ON THE NEXT ROLL OF THE DICE (or one roll) and you will get paid 30 to 1. (Ask some mathematician to give you a better answer. I'm only a crapshooter, but if you want to emulate the ROAD GAME GRIND, (and have the patience) then make this a ONE ROLL BET.)

Your Betting Stake in Lay Betting $51 to win $25 against a minimum of 10 shooters would be $510. Let YOUR total gambling bankroll tell you how big a stake to use. On a 1 to 10 scale, how do I rate this as a ONE ROLL PLAY?? About 6½. As an ALL DAY PLAY?? (Or until a win/loss decision is reached.) I think it stinks!! But walk from table to table, and you'll find most Wrong Bettors making it an ALL DAY BET.

Here is a similar play that I've PERSONALLY had pretty good results with. I LAY BET $31 to $25 for ONE ROLL ONLY against the 6 or the 8. My 10 bet issue is $310 instead of $510 required for the 4 or 10 bet. Depending at which end of the table I'm at, I Lay Bet against the 6 or 8 that is closest to my end.

Want my advice? LAY BET the $31 to win $25 for the ONE ROLL ONLY!!

THE SUCCESSFUL WRONG BETTOR

To have any chance of becoming a successful Wrong or Backline Bettor at CASINO CRAPS, the number one rule is that YOU NEVER CHASE A LOSING BET. You don't fade a shooter for two passes or three passes. You don't even fade a shooter for two NATURALS (7 or 11). That's right!! A Natural on the Come-out Roll and you are off this shooter. ONE Pass Line Point that the shooter makes, and you are finished with this shooter. You must now wait for the NEXT shooter before you make your NEXT bet.

You don't need a college degree in common sense to admit that a shooter who can beat you for ONE BET, could possibly beat you for TWO or THREE or even TWENTY-THREE BETS!! How many bets can the Wrong Bettor beat ANY ONE shooter for??

You might have to wait for 2 minutes or 22 minutes for the shooter to seven-out. The following shooter could do the same thing. This could go on and on.

Let's assume that you are at a four or five hour stag or floating crap game, or a four or five day gambling junket. Do you honestly think that you would have the patience to sweat out these hands?? After more than 50 years as a craps player and crap game employee, I unfortunately feel that your chances of successfully handling the Wrong or Backline side of the crap table is very slight.

In man to man fade games, it's a different game altogether. You don't have the BAR POINTS (1-1 or 6-6 depending on where you are playing.) You don't have to pay the 5% VIGORISH or COMMISSION to TAKE or LAY the odds, when you don't have an EVEN MONEY FLAT BET. Who knows?? You may still be able to steal an EVEN MONEY bet against the 6 or 8!! (Who pays the TRUE ODDS in a private or Army crap game?)

In spite of these advantages, the number of successful Wrong Bettors are still not that plentiful . . . IMPATIENCE . . . LACK OF TIME . . . ENVY . . . will very often cause the BACKLINE BILLIES to either switch to the Pass Line side, or tap himself out by "TAKING THE STEAM" and chasing down a Hand or Shoot. It's not too hard to make a Right Bettor out of a Wrong Bettor . . . but it's almost impossible to make a Wrong Bettor out of a Right Bettor.

And now . . . let us see whether I can be of some help in developing a few of the rarest of all crapshooters . . . THE SUCCESSFUL WRONG BETTOR.

Although I don't like your chances, I at least hope to prevent you from remaining, (if you are now) or becoming, (if you are not now) a CHARLIE CHASE. This is the player who can win one bet on a shooter . . . or could . . . by chasing down a hand . . . lose 3, 5, 10 or more bets on another shooter.

The various methods of play that I will describe for the Wrong Bettor, have the merit to be played for money. (Not matches.)

They range from the CONSERVATIVE BASIC STRATEGY PLAY, to the highly speculative FAST ACTION PLAY for the take-a-shot player. I may from time to time sound like a broken record, but one betting rule I will continually repeat . . . YOU NEVER CHASE A LOSING BET!!

I should qualify this by saying that in ALL my methods of play (except the Basic Strategy Play for the Wrong Bettor) that PART BETS are a portion of a COMPLETE BET. Unlike systems where you CHASE LOSSES with increased size bets from your BETTING STAKE, we on the other hand increase the size of OUR PART BETS from WINNING BETS ONLY. (Until a NET WIN or a COMPLETE LOSS is reached.) I'll explain these moves much fuller as we go along.

The money numbers (or amounts) that we will be using, will be for the SINGLE ODDS CASINOS. The reason being, that they are as yet more common throughout the world than casinos that deal DOUBLE or TRIPLE or better odds.

The using of my STOP LOSS MOVES for the Wrong Bettor, are of much more value in MULTIPLE ODDS CASINOS. This does not work as well for the Right Bettor.

THE BASIC STRATEGY PLAY FOR THE WRONG BETTOR

This method of play for the Wrong Bettor, is the least nerve-racking of the different Wrong or Backline Plays. The conservative betting progression (averaging approximately 20%) is in contrast to the approximately 50% increase in winning bets of the Basic Strategy Play for the right Bettor. The reason for the difference in the increase of winning bets is obvious. As a Right Bettor you GET or TAKE the odds. (Your investment is LESS.) As a Wrong Bettor, you GIVE or LAY the odds. (Your investment is MORE.)

This Basic Strategy Play requires a total Betting Stake of 30 times your minimum Don't Pass Line Bet. A $5 bettor would require a Betting stake of $150. A $25 bettor would require a $750 Betting Stake. These Betting Stakes are for the SINGLE ODDS BETTOR. The Double Odds Bettor would require 50 times your minimum size bet.

FOLLOWING ARE THE BETTING RULES

(1) Place your Betting Stake in the FRONT or BETTING PORTION of the check rack. We wait for a NEW shooter to get the dice. You NEVER bet into a started hand.

(2) Make your bet on the Don't Pass Line.

(3) If a Pass Line Point is rolled (4-5-6-8-9-10), lay the odds.

(4) If a LIVE or PAYOFF CRAPS is rolled, (1-1, 1-2 where these pay off, or 1-2, 6-6 where THESE pay off) you PARLAY or let ride the entire bet. Should a second consecutive LIVE CRAP be rolled, then your parlay is now complete and you increase the following bet to the next higher level.

Should the shooter roll ONE live crap and then roll a Box Point (4-5-6-8-9-10) you would NOT LAY THE ODDS. In so doing, you are salvaging the odds portion that was earmarked for this bet, and still have a 3 to 1 bet going for you. Parlaying live crap rolls is the smartest bet on the crap table for the Wrong Bettor. Besides salvaging the Lay Odds Portion of a bet, the parlays on these crap rolls help to overcome the 7s and 11s that are the enemy of the Wrong Bettor. Playing DOUBLE or TRIPLE ODDS you would go for a 3 WAY PARLAY, instead of just the 2 ways that you use in Single Odds. The same goes for the TRIPLE, QUADRUPLE or QUINTUPLE ODDS dealt at the VEGAS CLUB, also the QUINTUPLE ODDS dealt at BOB STUPAK'S VEGAS WORLD on the STRIP. As for the 10 to 1 ODDS dealt at BENNY BINION'S HORSESHOE CASINO, go for a 4 WAY PARLAY. Any parlay would of course start with a LIVE or PAYOFF CRAP ROLL plus the extra crap rolls. (Or box numbers that you DON'T lay the odds on.)

(5) Should a Natural (7 or 11) be rolled, you would NOT make any further bets against THIS Shooter. (Until the next time around? Not for life!!) Again children, remember that YOU NEVER CHASE A LOSING BET. I've had it happen while betting Wrong, that 9 consecutive shooters rolled either a 7 or 11 on their Come-out Roll. Nine consecutive times I cursed under my breath, folded my arms and waited for a New shooter. I swear on a stack that it was almost an hour before I had a live bet in action . . . And you want to become a successful Wrong Bettor?? I don't envy you your chances. LACK OF TIME . . . LACK OF PATIENCE . . . ENVY in watching a big Hand or Shoot take place while your arms are folded, are the main reasons that aside from my "PENSIONER and MRS. DICE DOCTOR PLAYERS" there aren't a half dozen successful Wrong Bettors in all of Las Vegas. As for Atlantic City, I have as yet to see a

Wrong Bettor that PLAYS FOR KEEPS.* (*Without taking the steam and chasing.)

(6) On the last bet left in your Betting Stake, you may if necessary take enough from your lock-up checks to properly complete that ONE bet.

(7) When we have played out the Betting Stake, we count the lock-up chips. Should we find that we have enough (both winnings and Betting Stake combined) to move up to our next higher level (approximately 20%), we do so and pocket or cash in the balance.

Should we find that we've shown a profit of ANY amount, but less than enough to move up to our next higher betting level, we STILL remain at the same table. You NEVER leave a table that has shown a profit on your Betting Stake. Don't laugh!! There are plenty of crapshooters with ants in their pants, that can't stand to stay in one spot, even when they are winning. Don't ask me why. I'm a crapshooter, not a SHRINK. Maybe they got a tip from one of the dealers that a hot hand is due.

Should you show a loss on your Betting Stake, you would move on to the next consecutively numbered table. You would again issue your minimum size Betting Stake.

P.S. Let me again show you how to arrive at the size of your STARTING Betting Stake. As an occasional player, don't use more than 5% of your **TOTOL GAMBLING** BANKROLL. As a PRO or everyday player, 1 or 2% of your TOTAL GAMBLING BANKROLL will keep you in action for the rest of your life . . . PROVIDING YOU PLAY FOR KEEPS.

At the end of a day's gambling, (regardless as to whether you have won or lost) take a count of your Total Gambling Bankroll. This is what you will NOW use as a figure to determine the size of your Betting Stake for the NEXT session.

When the professional or successful gambler reaches a predetermined size to his TOTAL GAMBLING BANKROLL he will invest any extra monies into other non-gambling investments. (Which should automatically eliminate the STOCK MARKET.) These investments could include property for your personal use. Collectables that will give you pleasure, such as paintings, antiques, a second home where you've always wanted to spend some time of the year at. In other words, anything you enjoy having or doing EXCEPT gambling.

(8) Here is how you arrive at the amount of your lock-up checks. For example: You are a $10 bettor. You bet $10 on the Don't Pass Line and the shooter rolls a 9. You lay $15 in odds. You win your bet and receive a total payoff of $45. Your next bet would be $12. (Approximately a 20% increase in the size of your bet, or easier yet, the bettor who starts with a $10 bet would increase his winning bets by $2 each. The $25 bettor would increase his winning bets by $5 each.)

On your increased bet of $12, the shooter rolls a 10, and you lay $24 in odds to win another $12. On winning your previous bet on the 9, you received $45. Of this $45, you used $36 to cover your new bet on the 10. This leaves a balance of $9 that you place into the lock-up rack. In other words after winning a bet and then completing the following INCREASED bet, we place whatever remains into the REAR or LOCK-UP PORTION of the CHIP RACK.

(9) Here is how you arrive at your next higher Betting Stake Level:
As a $10 plus odds bettor, your Betting Stake would be $300. For the $12 plus odds bettor, the stake is $360. For the $14 bettor the stake is $420. Etc., etc.

The $25 bettor would increase his winning bets by $5 plus odds. The $100 bettor increases his winning bets by $25 each plus odds.

THE 100% GUARANTEED WINNING BET

The most immature and disgusting remark you will ever hear at a Crap Table, is a Wrong Bettor calling "NO ACTION", when he is betting on the Don't Pass or the Don't Come Line, and the shooter rolls a 6 or an 8.

I have seen and heard these NO ACTION calls on $5 bets, on $50 and $100 bets, and in one case on $500 and $1000 bets by a (formerly) well known hi-roller at the Boardwalk Regency Casino in Atlantic City. In this case, this NO ACTION player's own brother gave me $10,000 to BOOK (or take over) the bets on the 6 and 8 that this dummy gave back to the House for NOTHING. I don't care whether this player reads this or not. After I went to the trouble of explaining the right moves regarding the advantage of AT LEAST hedging these bets on his NO ACTION CALLS, he stupidly told me it wasn't worth his time to bother, and that he would continue playing the same way. He just wouldn't get it through his thick skull that the Wrong Bettor prays he can avoid running into a 7 or an 11 when he makes a Don't Pass or a Don't Come Bet. Does he have to put himself through DOUBLE JEOPARDY by making this NO ACTION call, then turn around and make the same Don't Pass or Don't Come Bet over again??

This particular play, together with a few other weak moves, has sent this player to the BRICK WALL. (Tap city, BROKE!!) He has since moved to Arizona. When I saw him in action in the winter of 1982 he was playing at a 25¢ crap table in downtown Vegas. He didn't see me, and I wouldn't embarrass this (former) millionaire hi-roller by letting him know that I saw the depths he had sunk to. (All because of the disgusting way in which he used his gambling money.)

Seeing these BRICK WALL CASES are unfortunately all too common. These players beat themselves for MUCH MORE than the House does. Simple arithmetic will show you that if you must make this IDIOT PLAY by calling NO ACTION, then at least HEDGE the bet and you will wind up making something, whether the point is made or not.

For example: You have a $25 bet AGAINST the point (6 or 8). You would now make a $24 PLACE BET on the SAME point. Your combined bet, FOR and AGAINST the point would now be $49. Should the shooter seven-out, you would receive $50 for a net profit of $1. Should the shooter make the point, you would receive a total payoff of $52, for a net profit of $3. Not much of a profit either way, but a hell of a lot better than taking another chance of running into the sheriff or his deputy, (the 7 or 11). Just remember that this sheriff's posse has 8 ways of grabbing you on the Come-out Roll, (six 7's and two 11's). You as a Wrong Bettor, have only 3 ways of beating him. Three LIVE or PAYOFF CRAP ROLLS. The fourth Crap Roll is a STANDOFF or BAR POINT. No win. No lose. If you are going to play like an IDIOT and call NO ACTION, then at least make this small change.

YOU WILL NOW BE PLAYING LIKE AN INTELLIGENT IDIOT!!

I don't recommend hedge bets on ANY numbers. It's only a cop-out for the GUTLESS WONDER that calls NO ACTION!! As stupid as this NO ACTION play is, it is FOUND MONEY for the Crap Table Hustler that can get a player to let him take over the bet. It's better to sell it to a fellow crapshooter, (hustler or not) rather than to give it up for the House for NOTHING.

When I titled this play THE 100% WINNING BET, I should have made a clearer reference to THE CRAP TABLE HUSTLER as being the guaranteed winner. For you, the actual player, take my word for it that THE HOUSE WILL CUT YOU A BRAND NEW ASS if as a Wrong Bettor, you continue to call NO ACTION!!

Win or lose, just remember and accept the FACT, that against the 6 or 8, you are a 6 to 5 FAVORITE to win. Against the 5 or 9, you are a 3 to 2 FAVORITE to win. Against the 4 or the 10, you are a 2 to 1 FAVORITE to win your bet.

Mike G., a well known writer on gambling, once wrote that a crapshooter died and took an unbeatable system to his grave. Bullshaloney Mike!! THIS is the 100% GUARANTEED WINNING SYSTEM. You and I have used this play for OUR more than 50 years at the crap table. And we know that WE didn't originate this play.

All you have to do is to find MORONS that call NO ACTION, and of course that the House doesn't object to your taking over their bets.

Any sarcasm or belittling remarks, in this or any other chapter I write, is definitely INTENTIONAL. I'm the Dice Doctor. My job is to try and help the weak crapshooter smarten up and learn how to PLAY FOR KEEPS.

If taking a little sarcasm will help you, IT'S A SMALL PRICE TO PAY. Take my word for it. I PAID MUCH MORE!

THE PENSIONER'S PLAY FOR THE WRONG BETTOR

About 30 years ago, an old timer I had befriended at the crap tables, asked me to come up with a play for the Wrong Bettor that he could handle with a very small bankroll. He was getting his Social Security and a small pension from the First World War.

After paying his month's rent and board, plus a few incidentals, he had about $40 left for pocket or gambling money. Since there was no shortage of 25¢ MINIMUM BET (and even the odd 10¢ table) crap tables in downtown Las Vegas, I came up with the following Method of Play. I chose to call this play the PENSIONER'S PLAY for the WRONG BETTOR.

Although I originally taught my pensioner friend how to play this method with 25¢ chips, it can naturally be played with $1, $5, $25 or $100 chips. The size of your individual betting units are up to you and your personal TOTAL GAMBLING BANKROLL. I pointed out to my friend that $40 a month was a very small gambling bankroll. He agreed, but said since he had many times gone broke the day after he got his checks, that anything I might come up with, couldn't be much worse, and would probably be an improvement.

I had to agree, but at the same time insisted that he follow certain MONEY MANAGEMENT RULES I would outline. By following these money management rules, should he hit the BRICK WALL and the dice go completely against him, he could be in action at least 8 or 9 days of each month. Should the dice take their normal Law of Probabilities course, then it would be possible for him to not only be in action every day of the month, but even give him a chance to build up his gambling bankroll.

This was a GRIND SYSTEM that I had come up with and had personally used since 1931. Read the next chapter titled THE DADDY PLAY. In the PENSIONER'S PLAY I recommended a maximum of three (3) betting units on any one shooter. My Total Betting Stake would consist of 18 betting units.

FOLLOWING ARE THE MOVES IN THE PENSIONER'S PLAY

(1) Your Individual Betting Stake consists of three single betting units. (A single betting unit can be anywhere from a 25¢ chip and up.) Your TOTAL BETTING STAKE will be SIX times your INDIVIDUAL BETTING STAKE of THREE Betting units each. (In the case of my pensioner friend, his Total Betting Stake was 18 times 25¢, or $4.50.)

(2) Place the 18 chips in the FRONT or BETTING PORTION of your CHIP RACK.

(3) Hold three chips in your hand and wait for a NEW shooter to get the dice.

(4) Make your FIRST bet of one chip on the Don't Pass Line.

(5) Should the first roll of the dice be a Natural (7 or 11), you would make NO further bets against this shooter. (WE DON'T CHASE A LOSING BET.) You hold the remaining two chips and wait for a NEW shooter to get the dice. You may have to wait a minute or two, or you may have to wait for many minutes. It is also possible for 1, 2, 3 or more consecutive shooters to roll a Natural (7 or 11) on their come-out roll. Still want to become a Wrong Bettor??

(6) Should the shooter roll a LIVE or PAYOFF CRAP (1-1 or 1-2) in Las Vegas or Atlantic City, (6-6, 1-2) elsewhere, you would PARLAY (or double) the entire amount. You would continue parlaying any number of CONSECUTIVE LIVE (or payoff) CRAP ROLLS. In the case of the bigger bettor he would, after reaching the table limit, continue betting the LIMIT. As a Wrong Bettor, your best chance of overcoming the Naturals that show when you bet the Don't Pass or the Don't Come Lines, are in PARLAYING THESE PAYOFF CRAP ROLLS.

Let's continue with the two units we were holding. You bet one of the units on the Don't Pass Line. Should the shooter roll a BOX POINT (4-5-6-8-9-10), you would bet the remaining unit on the Don't Come Line. Should the shooter again roll an open box number, we would have two betting units in action against this shooter. (Remember?? We lost the first unit when the previous shooter rolled a Natural (7 or 11)).

The shooter sevens out and you receive a total payoff of four units for a net profit of one unit. You place this winning unit into the rear or lock-up portion of the chip rack. You keep the other three units in your hand and start over again on the next shooter. Should all three of your units be in single action and the shooter then miss out, you would receive a payoff of six units, for a net profit of three units that you lock up. Should you run into PARLAYS on LIVE CRAP ROLLS, then there is no limit (except table limits) on the number of units you could win on any one shooter.

(7) Should the shooter come out on a point, and on his second roll, and YOUR second bet, BUCK or repeat his point, you would NOT make a third bet against this shooter. Should the shooter now seven out, you would again have three units. (Two you received when the shooter sevened out, plus one unit you DIDN'T use when the shooter REPEATED his Pass Line Point on the SECOND roll.)

On the other hand, should the shooter again make the point you had covered, you would only have ONE unit remaining. You must now hope to run into enough miss-outs to get back your three units and again start playing for a profit. The quickest way of doing this would be to parlay your bet with this one unit, providing it is a winning roll. (One winning unit makes two. Two winning units makes four, for a net profit of ONE unit. Right?? Right!!)

(8) You can easily see that a shooter who can knock you out of THREE units, could just as easily, (IF YOU TAKE THE STEAM AND CHASE) knock you out of 13 or 33 units. The limiting of your loss on any one shooter, is an important part of the MOST important whole . . . YOUR MONEY MANAGEMENT.

Should you, after playing out your Betting Stake of 18 Units, show a profit of ANY amount, you would remain at the same table and start over again with the same 18 units. Should you show a LOSS on your 18 unit Betting Stake, you would move on to the next consecutively numbered table.

After testing different quantities as betting stakes, I found that the quantity I have recommended gives any one crap table a fair chance of something showing. It also prevents your jumping from table to table, looking for the COLD ONE. It is more than possible when you are all over the place, to leave one JUST TURNED COLD table after another. Do yourself a favor and keep this in mind . . . IT ONLY TAKES ONE ROLL OF THE DICE TO TURN A HOT TABLE TO ICE . . . AND VICE VERSA . . .

For the conservative man or woman player who has the TIME and the PATIENCE, I highly recommend this Wrong Betting Play.

THE DADDY PLAY FOR THE WRONG BETTOR

My reason for naming this the DADDY PLAY, was because it was the FIRST Wrong Betting Play that showed me a WINNING BATTING AVERAGE. (It is the FATHER of most of my later Wrong Betting Plays.)

I started with this play in the early thirties, when practically every state in the union had fairly wide-open gambling. (Horse books, craps, poker, etc.) If it wasn't by local option, then you pieced off the MAN and operated. Then as now, you might have to take a small vacation at election time, or when some do-gooders put up a big enough Hey Rube. Once in a very long time, you might even have to take a pinch. (Just to make it look good for the solid citizens.) If doing time was part of the pinch, then (at a price) there was always an available fall guy.

Although I've been a part of the crap game as a bettor and as a bookie, (employee, part or full owner of a floating crap game) and in spite of my biggest wins coming as a Right Bettor, I have as a player been basically a Wrong Bettor.

Many Wrong or Backline players may call this Method of Play pretty gutless. The reason being that in this play YOU DO NOT LAY THE ODDS. I partially agree. However, when you consider one of the moves, that of PARLAYING any number of CONSECUTIVE LIVE CRAP ROLLS, you will find that it takes more than just a bit of guts.

My record to date, has been 5 consecutive LIVE or PAYOFF crap rolls, a point and then a miss-out. I was at the time making $10 UNIT bets, and took down $640 for that ONE $10 bet. The point I had to overcome was an 8, so I wouldn't exactly call this a gutless method of play.

The Total Betting Stake required for this Method of Play is 36 Units of whatever size fits in with your TOTAL GAMBLING BANKROLL. It can be $1 chips, $5 chips, $25 chips, $100 chips or 25¢ chips. These 36 units are divided by 6.

The reason behind the Individual Betting Stake of 6 units is because of the 6 Box Points (4-5-6-8-9-10). The player hopes to cover all 6 Box Numbers without running into one of our STOP LOSS MOVES, and then have the shooter seven out.

After many thousands of hands in Live action, it has only happened to me twice. The first time was at a floating crap game in Oakville, Ontario, Canada. It was in 1954, and believe it or not, Hurricane Hazel was going on outside. (Sorry to hear that Jackie R., who ran the games, sevened-out in 1982. He was one of the classiest crap game operators around.)

The second time I ran into this clean sweep, was on opening day at Bally's Park Place Casino in Atlantic City in December of 1979. (You don't forget the dates and places of interesting events in the life of the crapshooter.) I have a few other times lined up all 6 Box Numbers, only to have the shooter pluck me off like a chicken. (One number (feather) at a time.) However, it takes much less than a clean sweep to show a net profit, on any one shooter.

O.K. Kids. Let's shoot craps. Following are the moves for the DADDY PLAY.

(1) You place the 36 Unit Betting Stake into the FRONT or BETTING PORTION of the CHIP RACK. You take and hold 6 Units in your hand, wait for a NEW shooter and then bet one (1) Unit on the Don't Pass Line. The shooter rolls a Natural (7 or 11). You make NO FURTHER BETS against this shooter. (Till the next time round. Successful Wrong Bettors don't chase a losing bet. Remember??) We are now holding 5 Betting Units in our hand and wait for a NEW shooter before we make our next bet.

(2) We bet one Unit on the Don't Pass Line. The shooter comes out on a LIVE (or payoff) Crap Roll. We parlay (or let ride) both units on the Don't Pass Line. The shooter rolls a Box Number (4-5-6-8-9-10). We now bet one Unit on the Don't Come Line and the shooter rolls an eleven (11). Since this is one of our STOP LOSS numbers, we make no further bets against this shooter. After a few more rolls, the shooter makes his point. We are now down to three (3) of our six (6) Units, and must wait for a NEW SHOOTER to get the dice before we start again with the 3 remaining Units.

(3) We bet one Unit on the Don't Pass Line and the shooter rolls a Box Number (4-5-6-8-9-10). We now bet one Unit on the Don't Come Line, and the shooter rolls a different Box Number. We bet the last of the three Units on the Don't Come Line, and the shooter again rolls a Box Point number that we had not already covered.

After a couple more rolls of the dice, the shooter sevens out and we receive a Total Payoff of six (6) Units. Which is what we had to start with, but since we are NOT here to break even, we will now try and use up all six Units on three (3) bets. Two Units on the Don't Pass Line and two Units each on two Don't Come Line Bets.

In this the DADDY PLAY as in all of my partial bet Wrong Plays, we must either show NET WIN DECISION of one or more units, or a loss of ALL 6 Units. It is quite possible for you to run into any number of net win decisions before you lose even ONE of your 6 Unit Betting Stakes.

(4) We bet TWO UNITS on the Don't Pass Line and the shooter rolls a LIVE (or payoff) CRAP. We PARLAY or let ride all 4 Units on the Don't Pass Line and the shooter rolls a Box Number. We now bet TWO UNITS on the Don't Come Line, and the shooter rolls a different Box Number. We bet the remaining TWO UNITS again on the Don't Come Line, and the shooter rolls a 7. The hand or shoot is now over.

We receive a payoff of 8 Units from the parlay on the Don't Pass Line, and another 4 Units from the bet we had on the Don't Come Line. From these 12 Units we place 6 Units into the REAR or LOCK-UP PORTION of the CHIP RACK. We again hold a 6 Unit Betting Stake in our hand and start over again with a ONE Unit bet on the NEXT shooter.

After playing out your 36 Unit TOTAL BETTING STAKE, should you show a net profit of ANY amount, you would remain at the same table and start over again. Should you show a LOSS on your Total Betting Stake, you would move on to the next consecutively numbered table.

As I mentioned at the start of this play, I have personally used it off and on for more than 50 years. I doubt you will run into a GRIND PLAY for the Wrong Bettor that is more relaxing. Try it. You'll like it.

THE TRUE COUNT PLAY FOR THE WRONG BETTOR

By using such wording as BASIC STRATEGY or TRUE COUNT when I refer to plays at the crap table, some blackjack authors or self-styled authorities may take offense. In case I haven't said it before, I'll say it now. Go sue me. I've used these wordings for almost 50 years, and when I saw these same wordings in print less than 25 years ago, when you referred to moves in blackjack, I didn't threaten YOU with court action.

In this play, keeping a TRUE COUNT is important enough for an error of even a single dollar, to cause the loss of a COMPLETE BETTING STAKE. Don't let this scare you. The mathematics used, as in all my methods of play, are simple 9 year-old arithmetic. At the same time even a 9 year-old makes mistakes, and in gambling THIS CAN BE FATAL. (You could blow the whole teppel schmaltz ... the woiks!!) As we go along, you will see why THE TRUE COUNT must be adhered to.

(1) Here is how you arrive at your TOTAL BETTING STAKE. Let us assume you are a $5 Bettor. You would require a Total Betting Stake of $80. You arrive at this $80 total in the following way: Six times $5 to cover the FLAT PORTION of six (6) possible points (4-5-6-8-9-10). This amounts to $30. You now add the ODDS PORTION you must LAY against the six Box Numbers ... $10 each against the 4 and 10 equals $20 ..

$9 each against the 5 and 9 equals $18 ... $6 each against the 6 and 8 equals $12. This makes the TOTAL LAY PORTION $50, and combined with the FLAT PORTION $80. For the $10 Bettor, your Total Betting Stake would be $154. (Yes it's an odd amount, but for the $10 Bettor it's the exact TRUE COUNT TOTAL to the last $1.) The $15 bettor requires $270. The $25 bettor requires $400. The $75 bettor requires $1350.

The 75¢ bettor requires $13.50. (Don't laugh at the 25¢ bettor. It's the gamble that you give your gambling money, not the size of your betting stake.) I've seen small money gamblers that were a pleasure to watch. I've seen hi-rollers that made me sick to the stomach with their weak play. I'll repeat . . . It's money you earmarked for gambling . . . give it a gambling chance . . .

(2) I have selected the $154 Betting Stake for the $10 Bettor. (Again your personal betting stake should depend on your TOTAL GAMBLING BANKROLL, and will fluctuate in size according to your wins and losses as you go along.) The occasional gambler should use about 5% for any one Betting Stake. The regular (or limited few professionals) will seldom use more than 1 or 2% of his TOTAL GAMBLING BANKROLL for any one session.

(3) We wait for a NEW shooter to get the dice and then make a $10 bet on the Don't Pass Line. (As a Wrong Bettor, you NEVER step into a hand or shoot where the shooter has made a pass or a Natural (7 or 11).

Should the shooter roll a Natural (7 or 11) on his Come-out Roll, we would NOT make any further bets against this shooter. (Again, as in all Wrong Betting, WE NEVER CHASE A LOSING BET.)

(4) Should the shooter roll a LIVE or PAYOFF CRAPS, 1-1 or 1-2, where they count, or 6-6 or 1-2, where THEY count, we PARLAY or let ride the entire $20. Should the shooter again roll a Live Crap, we would now parlay the $40. (We continue parlaying any number of Live crap rolls. Should you be a bigger bettor and reach the table limit, you would continue making limit bets.)

Getting back to our $40 parlay, should the shooter roll a Box Number (4-5-6-8-9-10), we would lay the odds against the entire $40. (Should you not have enough in your Betting Stake to completely cover the bet, you would Lay Bet as much as you DO have remaining in your Betting Stake.)

In this TRUE COUNT PLAY, it is possible to run into enough consecutive LIVE CRAP ROLLS to use your entire Betting Stake against a SINGLE NUMBER. Win or lose, YOU have the edge and it is therefore an extra bonus when you run into these Live Crap Rolls. In addition, these crap rolls when parlayed, help overcome the Naturals (7 or 11) that the Wrong Bettor so often runs into.

(5) We now make a bet on the Don't Come Line. Should the shooter roll a new point, we Lay Bet the Odds and again make a bet on the Don't Come Line. We continue making bets on the Don't Come Line as long as we don't run into a repeat of a number we already have covered, or an eleven (11). Both of which are STOPPERS or STOP LOSS NUMBERS. Of course, should the shooter roll a SEVEN, then this Hand or Shoot is over. The shooter could also line us up behind some numbers and then proceed to knock us off, one number at a time, so that by the time the shooter sevens out, we could be plucked clean.

(6) Here are a few more moves that you might run into during the TRUE COUNT PLAY.

Example #1: You make a $10 bet on the Don't Pass Line. The shooter rolls a 9, and you LAY $15 against the 9 to win another $10. You now make a $10 bet on the Don't Come Line, and the shooter rolls a 7. You have bet off a total of $35 and you receive a payoff of $45. This gives you a NET PROFIT of $10 which you place into the REAR or LOCK-UP PORTION of the CHIP RACK.

Example #2: You bet $10 on the Don't Pass Line and the shooter rolls an 8. You LAY $12 against the 8 to win another $10. You now bet $10 on the Don't Come Line and the shooter rolls a 4. You LAY $20 in Odds against the 4 to win another $10. You make another $10 Don't Come Line bet and the shooter rolls a 7. You lose that $10 bet and the hand is over. The dealer pays you $42 for your bet against the 8, and he pays you $50 for your bet against the 4, for a total payoff of $92. The cost to you for these bets was $62 which gives you a NET PROFIT of $30 that you place into the lock-up rack. Taking a quick count, will verify that your Betting Stake is again at $154.

Example #3: You bet $10 on the Don't Pass Line, and the shooter rolls an 8. You LAY $12 against the 8 to win another $10. You now bet $10 on the Don't Come Line and the shooter rolls a 4. You LAY $20 in Odds against the 4 to win another $10. You make another $10 bet on the Don't Come Line and the shooter rolls an 11. You lose this $10 bet, and DO NOT MAKE ANY FURTHER BETS against this shooter. You must now wait in hopes that the shooter will seven out before he makes either the 4 or the 8, or both. Unfortunately he makes them both. Your loss on this shooter is $62, coming from a $22 loss against the 8, a $30 loss agaisnt the 4, and a $10 loss when the 11 showed against your 2nd bet on the Don't Come Line.

Your Betting Stake has been reduced to $92. You must now start over against the NEXT shooter with your reduced Betting Stake of $92. I have many times (during this play) been down to a few dollars, and then have the dice turn for me to where I not only got back my entire Betting Stake, but went on to getting back into the money-winning action. (Or as we crapshooters should know and accept: AS LONG AS YOU HAVE THE PRICE OF A LAYDOWN (a bet) YOU ARE STILL IN ACTION.

My personal record of making a comeback, took place at the Riviera Hotel on the Strip. I was down to $2 from a $154 Betting Stake. Fortunately the table I was playing at had a $2 Minimum Table Limit. I ran into seven (7) consecutive miss-outs and Live Crap Rolls. Starting with my last $2 on the Don't Pass Line, I increased my winning bets as follows: 2-4-8-16-32-64-128 and $256. I not only got back my $154 Betting Stake, but locked up an additional $102 profit. I almost turned purple waiting for the last two miss-outs. (I'M NOT A COMPLETE ROBOT.)

Example #4: We continue: The balance of our Betting Stake is $92. We must now try and come from behind and get into the black (or winning side). We bet $10 on the Don't Pass Line and the shooter comes out on an 8. We lay $12 in odds behind the 8. We now bet $10 on the Don't Come Line, and the shooter rolls a 4. We lay $20 in odds behind the 4. We again bet $10 on the Don't Come Line, and the shooter comes out on an eleven (11).

Since the 11 is one of our STOP LOSSES, we make NO FURTHER BETS against this shooter. The shooter now sevens out, and we get a total payoff of $92. We made a net profit of $30 on this shooter, bringing our Betting Stake up to $122. Now comes the tricky part. We are still trying to get back to our $154 Betting Stake, plus a profit (if it's meant to be).

We are still a loser on our Betting Stake, but since we DID show a profit on the last shooter, we now bet $20 on the Don't Pass Line and any following Don't Come Line bets.

Example #5: We bet $20 on the Don't Pass Line. The shooter rolls a Live Crap (1-1 or 1-2). We now have $40 on the Don't Pass Line. We PARLAY or let ride the $40 and the shooter comes out on an 8. We lay $60 in Odds to win $50. (Which we are permitted to do in a Single Odds game.) We now bet $20 on the Don't Come Line, and the shooter rolls a 4. Normally we could lay $40 in odds behind the 4. However, in our case, we have only $22 remaining in our Betting Stake from the $122 we had when this shooter started. We therefore lay the remaining $22 to win $11 against the 4.

As I have already mentioned, you will run into the odd tricky move, and it is at these times that you will see the importance of keeping a TRUE COUNT. Had the Don't Come Point have been a 5 or a 9, you would have layed $21 to win $14 and have just held on to the remaining $1. Had the Don't Come Point have been a 6 or an 8, you could have layed $18 to win $15, and bet the remaining $4 on the Don't Come Line. (In plain English, we put every dollar into action that we can. I am also assuming that we are at a $2 Minimum Betting Table, otherwise we would not be able to use any small pieces of money.)

Continuing with example #5: The shooter has sevened out and we receive a total payoff of $263, which came from $190 on the 8, and $73 on the 4. This permitted us to place $109 into the lock-up rack, and again have a $154 Betting Stake to continue with.

The TRUE COUNT PLAY (during my personal use of it for almost 45 years) has had a winning Batting Average for me. You MUST however, be mature enough to accept that ONE SHOOTER could conceivably line you up behind enough numbers to use up your entire Betting Stake, and then one by one, proceed to knock off EVERY NUMBER that you are behind. It is not common, but it can and does happen. It has happened to me A GREAT MANY TIMES.

The True Count Play, as in most of my methods of play, has been put together with the main goal being to give the House as little edge as possible. In Single Odds 4/5 of 1%. In Double Odds 3/5 of 1%, etc. TRIPLE ODDS are becoming commonplace in both Las Vegas and Atlantic City. You can even get up to 10 TIMES ODDS at BENNY BINION'S HORSESHOE CASINO in downtown Las Vegas. The VEGAS CLUB, also in downtown Las Vegas are dealing 3/4/5 ODDS. TRIPLE ODDS on 4 and 10. QUADRUPLE ODDS on 5 and 9. QUINTUPLE ODDS on 6 and 8.

If you are a Wrong or Backline Bettor and want the best advice money can buy, use my STOP LOSS MOVES and lay the MOST odds that the House will allow.

THE FAST ACTION PLAY FOR THE WRONG BETTOR

This play for the Wrong Bettor has a HIGH FATALITY RATE . . . on the other hand (if your nerves can take it), the big returns and the fast action is there. As a matter of fact, it is the closest to a TAKE A SHOT method of play, that I DO approve of. I have a number of reasons why, although I may approve of this method of play, I certainly don't recommend it for the fainthearted or gutless crapshooter. The arguments FOR the method are:

(1) We are giving the House less than a 1% edge.
(2) It has the big excitement for the fast action player.
(3) It can pay dividends for a small investment.

The reasons for being AGAINST it are:

(1) It can make a nervous wreck out of you.

(2) It can make a nervous wreck out of you.

(3) It can make a nervous wreck out of you.

Due to the high fatality rate, it is advisable for even the so-called high roller to cut down on the size of his individual betting stakes. After testing different sets of individual betting units, I found that the three-unit Betting Stake was the best. I also found that six (6) of these betting stakes (win or lose) gave any one Crap Table a FAIR CHANCE at something showing.

You will recall that in the PENSIONER'S PLAY, we also allowed three individual betting units for each betting stake. Six of these betting stakes made up the TOTAL BETTING STAKE. In the Pensioner's Play, we made FLAT BETS ONLY. (We did NOT lay the odds.) In this Fast Action Method of Play, WE DO LAY THE ODDS. Therefore our total investment is almost TRIPLE the amount required for the Pensioner's Play.

For example: The $5 Fast Action player would require a TOTAL BETTING STAKE of $264, or six (6) individual betting stakes of $44 each, to cover three (3) individual betting units.

The $10 bettor requires a total betting stake of $510.

The $15 bettor requires a total betting stake of $810.

The $25 bettor requires a total betting stake of $1,320.

Divide the TOTAL BETTING STAKE by six (6) to arrive at the amount of the INDIVIDUAL BETTING STAKES, which in turn will cover three (3) INDIVIDUAL BETTING UNITS.

In this FAST ACTION PLAY we use a much faster increase or progression in our winning bets (approximately 50%) than we do in our BASIC STRATEGY PLAY for the Wrong Bettor (approximately 20%).

The approximate 50% increase in winning bets is as follows:

5-7-10-15-25-35-50-75-125-175-250-350-500-700-1000-1500-2500-etc.

These are the FLAT PORTION of the Don't Pass or Don't Come Bets. Add to these the FULL SINGLE ODDS. Should you have access to a Double Odds Casino and wish to LAY THE DOUBLE ODDS, then you must figure out your bets and betting stake accordingly. There is a definite edge for the Wrong Bettor in being able to lay Double Odds over laying the Single Odds. It is much more so, in using our STOP LOSSES, the 7 and 11, or a repeated box number. (Some casinos are dealing TRIPLE ODDS and more.)

Following are the moves (or mechanics) of the FAST ACTION method of play for the WRONG BETTOR. The amounts we will work with will be that of the $10 bettor.

(1) We place the TOTAL BETTING STAKE of $510 in the rear portion of the chip rack. This $510 Total Betting Stake breaks down to six individual THREE UNIT BETTING STAKES of $85 each.

(2) We take $85 (or ONE Individual Betting Stake) and place it in the front or betting portion of the chip rack. This will be one of the six INDIVIDUAL betting stakes that we will be working with. Since we will be using the rear portion of the chip rack for any possible winnings, it will be up to you to keep the betting stakes and the lock-up (or winning chips) separate. You could keep the TOTAL betting stake in your pockets and take out ONE individual betting stake at a time. The reason I'm making such an issue of this, is because it is a very fast method of play, and it would be quite easy to make a mistake.

(3) As in all our methods of play for the Wrong Bettor, we wait for a NEW SHOOTER. We now make a $10 bet on the Don't Pass Line. Should the shooter roll a 7 or an 11 on the come-out roll, we would make NO further bets against THIS shooter. The 7 or 11 rolled on the come-out roll of EITHER the Don't Pass Line bet or the Don't Come Line bet, acts as our STOPPER or STOP LOSS MOVE.

Regardless as to whether we are betting our original $10 bet, or whether we have reached the Table Limit, anytime we run into a STOPPER or STOP LOSS MOVE, when we make our bet on a NEW SHOOTER it is always with our minimum bet. (Or as in our case $10.)

(4) We again make a $10 bet on the Don't Pass Line. The shooter comes out on a point, (4-5-6-8-9-10) and we Lay the Full Odds. We now bet $10 on the Don't Come Line, and the shooter rolls another point. (A different point than the one we already have covered on the Don't Pass Line.) We again lay the full odds. (In this play, we always lay the VERY MOST that the House will allow, or the most that we have remaining in our Betting Stake, should it be less than the full odds allowed.)

Now, providing that we haven't run into a repeat of one of the numbers we already have covered, or a STOPPER (the 7 or 11), or a LIVE (or payoff) CRAP ROLL, this is the third and LAST bet we would make against this shooter. In other words, the MOST bets that we will cover on any one shooter will be the Don't Pass Line and TWO Don't Come Line bets.

(5) Or this could happen: We make a $10 Don't Pass Line bet and the shooter rolls a Live or Payoff Craps. We would now have $20 on the Don't Pass Line (or the Don't Come Line, whichever). We parlay or let ride the entire $20, and the shooter rolls a point (4-5-6-8-9-10). We would now Lay the FULL ODDS against the ENTIRE $20. (It is quite possible, in this Fast Action Play, to run into enough consecutive Live Crap Rolls, to use your entire Individual Betting Stake against a SINGLE POINT or number.) This is the BEST possible thing that can happen for the Wrong Bettor. (Remember the $640 I picked up for a $10 bet, after I ran into five consecutive Live Crap Rolls and then a miss-out. This was in my DADDY PLAY and I didn't even have to Lay the Odds.)

It is a well known fact, whether you are a Right or a Wrong Bettor, that it is to your advantage to have as few bets as possible in action. Let me explain this a bit further, by saying that in the case of the Right Bettor, the more bets you have spread out on the table, the more individual winning rolls of the dice you must get just to cover your investment on this one shooter, let alone show a profit. To top it off, as a Right Bettor, you MUST accept the fact that a seven at the WRONG TIME can lose you anywheres from ONE to as many as more than TWENTY bets at one time. (Don't laugh!! You could have all of the following bets covered: The Pass Line plus Odds. All the other 5 Box Numbers. Six (6) Come Bets plus odds. All the 4 Hardways. All the 4 Horn Bet Numbers. The Big Red (7). The Field bet. And just to make it a little more IDIOTIC or STUPID, he could even have some HOP BETS going at the same time. Listen children. In my 58 years as an employee and as a player, I've seen this happen!)

As a Wrong or Backline Bettor, your main object is to avoid the 7 or 11 on the Come-out Roll on either the Don't Pass or the Don't Come Line. Once you do get behind one or more numbers, you are (win or lose) a favorite to win your bet or bets. In your case as a Wrong Bettor, a seven (7) at the RIGHT TIME can win you anywheres from one to six bets. (Or as in our case with the FAST ACTION PLAY, we could win anywheres from one to three bets.)

(6) The shooter sevens out, and whether we have won or lost money on this shooter is immaterial only as far as our next bet is concerned. Although we would like to show a win against every shooter when he sevens out. It is quite possible for us to be behind two or three numbers and then have the shooter repeat one or two of them. As long as we DO win at least ONE bet against this shooter, we increase the size of our next bet.

(7) Our next move is to make a $15 bet on the Don't Pass Line. We follow all the moves that we made with our $10 bet, except that we are on our next higher betting level. The shooter rolls a point and we Lay the Odds. We now make a $15 bet on the Don't Come Line. (It is quite possible at times not to have enough in your betting stake to make a full Don't Come Bet. In these cases you would bet whatever amount that you DO have in your Betting Stake. (Remember? Every buck in action that you can!!!)

There will also be times when the OPPOSITE will take place. This can happen when you run into an extra big payoff from Live Crap Rolls, at which time you will have more than enough in your Betting Stake to make more than your three bets. (The Don't Pass Line Bet plus the two Don't Come Bets.) You STILL make only three bets.

(8) Now, let us say that one or more consecutive shooters seven out, leaving us with something to collect (win or lose) on each of them. For example: We bet $10 on the Don't Pass Line and the shooter rolls an 8. We lay the $12 to $10 in Odds. We make a second bet of $10 on the Don't Come Line and the shooter rolls a 5. We Lay the $15 to $10 in Odds. We make a second Don't Come Bet and the shooter rolls a seven. This hand is finished. We won $20 on the 8 and $20 on the 5. We lost $10 when the shooter sevened out on our second Don't Come Bet. This leaves us with a temporary profit of $30 on this shooter. (The amount of profit is temporary since it's quite possible for us to lose it on a future bet that is part of a string of bets that are in ACTION until a net win or lose decision is reached. We are just hoping that one of our STOP LOSSES will come at the RIGHT TIME.

Since we DID get something back (win or lose) from the previous shooter, we increase the size of our bet or bets on the following shooter. We now bet $15 on the Don't Pass Line. The shooter rolls a seven and the hand or shoot is over (for us). Remember?? We no chase losing bets!!

We now take a quick (or slow) count of our Betting Stake and find that we have $15 over and above our original Betting Stake of $85. We place this $15 into the lock-up rack and wait for a NEW shooter before we start again with a $10 bet on the Don't Pass Line.

Another example: We have had four consecutive shooters seven out, after which we had at least one winning bet remaining. Whether we won or lost on any of these consecutive miss-outs is for the moment immaterial as far as our play is concerned. We did get back SOMETHING after each miss-out. We therefore increased the betting on these four consecutive miss-outs as follows: $10-$15-$25-$35 and $50. On the $50 bet the shooter rolled a Natural (7 or 11) on his Come-out Roll, and our win streak is at an end. Since our Betting Stake now contains more than our original $85, we place any amount over the $85 into the lock-up rack. We start over again on the NEXT new shooter with a $10 bet. (Or whatever YOUR minimum bet is.)

(9) We now come to the end of our TOTAL BETTING STAKE of six INDIVIDUAL Betting Stakes. As a $10 Bettor we started with a Total Betting Stake of $510. The $15 Bettor would require a Total Betting Stake of $810 consisting of SIX (6) INDIVIDUAL

BETTING STAKES OF $135 EACH.

On counting our lock-up chips, should we find that we have $810 or more, we would pocket or cash in anything over the $810. We remain at the same table and start out by making $15 initial or minimum bets. Should we have shown a profit of ANY AMOUNT over the original $510, we would STILL remain at the same table and start over again with our original $510 Betting Stake. (On a LOSS of any amount, we would move on to the next consecutively numbered table, and again start out with our minimum Betting Stake of $510. (Or whatever YOUR minimum is.)

In this FAST ACTION method of play it is highly possible to have enough in your lock-up rack to move up more than one level. However, we are adhering to our Betting Rules. One of which definitely says that YOU MOVE UP ONE LEVEL AT A TIME. (Besides, WE'VE GOT IT---LET THE HOUSE TRY AND GET IT BACK!!)

It does give you a good feeling, when you as DAVID, has the House as GOLIATH, by the BAYTSIM*. (*Nuts in Norwegian). It doesn't hurt just once in a while to hear the PIT PERSONNEL talking to themselves. (Must it ALWAYS be the players??)

My recommending the PARLAYING of LIVE or PAYOFF crap rolls does lose some of it's strength when playing in MULTIPLE ODDS games. However, even ONE payoff craps roll does act as a STOP LOSS in that you DO salvage the odds portion that you had earmarked for this bet. (Besides, ain't you never seen three, four or five consecutive miss-outs with the odd crap roll thrown in??)

In a Single Odds game, a NATURAL (7 or 11) on the come-out roll, would cost the Wrong Bettor between 33% to almost 50% of his full bet. In a Double Odds game, he could lose between 20% to almost 35% of his full bet. In a Triple, Quintuple or 10 Odds game?? You can easily see how little of your total bet you would lose, should the shooter come out on your STOP LOSS MOVE: A NATURAL.

For the Right Bettor, (unless he takes advantage of Naturals, 7 or 11), the multiple odds, (double, triple, quintuple or better) are more of a hindrance than a help. Granted, that mathematically, multiple odds for the Right Bettor does cut down on the House Edge against him. However, at the crap table it's a different story. Once a point is established, the Right Bettor must accept the FACT that he is a 6 to 5, a 3 to 2, or a 2 to 1 UNDERDOG. (The Wrong Bettor is in exactly the opposite position. HE is now (win or lose) the 6 to 5, 3 to 2, or the 2 to 1 FAVORITE to win his bet.)

There is one type of Right Bettor that could benefit from Multiple Odds. That would be the Come Line Bettor. For the past 3 years, I have table tested in LIVE action, the use of multiple odds (triple odds or better) for both the Right and the Wrong Bettor. By using my STOP LOSS MOVES, and proper MONEY MANAGEMENT, I found that betting Wrong showed an exceptional winning Batting Average.

However, as I've already mentioned, the Come Line Bettor using the multiple odds and being satisfied to GRIND, also showed a pretty good winning Batting Average. The main advantage for the Come Line Bettor using Multiple Odds, is that the FLAT or COME LINE PORTION of the total bet was so much less than the Flat or Come Line Portion of the Single Odds Bettor.

We all know that the Come Line Bettor's nemesis or enemy is the 7 on the Come-out Roll for a NEW Pass Line Point. The use of a smaller Flat Bet on the Come Line, together with the taking of Multiple Odds (double, triple, quintuple or better), helps to overcome this obstacle.

MY EXPENSE MONEY PLAY . . . WHEN BETTING WRONG

I don't want you to get the wrong impression, when I call this my EXPENSE MONEY PLAY. To many crapshooters, this could mean that I am trying to grind out a day's wages. Granted, there have been many days when I would have gladly settled for the day's nut (or expenses) but that was after I wound up a blank. (No wages today.) At other times I made the day's wages, the month's wages, and even more. At just one session.

In other words children, I WILL limit how much I could possibly LOSE at any one session, but I'll NEVER limit how much I can WIN. I WILL walk away with the crap table AND the casino, if the dice should go my way. (Why many gamblers are actually afraid to win, is one question mark I still haven't found an answer to.)

The EXPENSE MONEY PLAY should be used in casinos that deal at least DOUBLE ODDS. The STOP LOSS MOVES I use, will show you the advantage of MULTIPLE ODDS (double, triple, quintuple or more) over SINGLE ODDS, in this method of play.

Our first move is to decide on the size of our TOTAL BETTING STAKE. In my case, I use a minimum daily Betting Stake of $420. I divide this $420 by six (6) to give myself six THREE UNIT INDIVIDUAL BETTING STAKES of $70 each. Which means that $70 is the most I could possibly use (or lose) on any ONE shooter. Should I not use the full $70 on any one shooter, then I would hold the balance until I used it on a following shooter (if necessary) or lock it up if it becomes part of a winning bet without it actually being used. O.K. children. Let's shoot craps!!

Just remember that neither I nor anyone else can give you a written guarantee on any play at the Crap Table. However, for me this play has had a WINNING BATTING AVERAGE. It is slow. Often tedious and nerve-wracking. But if you have the PATIENCE (as you must have in any form of Wrong or Backline Betting), then I believe you will be pleased with the winning results.

(1) We wait for a NEW shooter to get the dice, and then bet $5 on the Don't Pass Line.

(2) Should the shooter roll a Natural (7 or 11), we make NO further bets against this shooter. (WE NEVER CHASE A LOSING BET!!)

(3) Should the shooter roll a LIVE or PAYOFF CRAPS (1-1 or 1-2 where these pay off, or 6-6 or 1-2 where THESE pay off) we PARLAY or let ride the ENTIRE $10. Should the shooter again roll a Live Crap, we would parlay the entire $20. Should the shooter now roll a Box Number (or Pass Line Point 4-5-6-8-9-10), we would Lay Bet the Odds against the $20. (Unless there was not enough remaining in our Betting Stake to lay FULL ODDS. In which case we lay bet whatever we DO have.)

It is possible in this play to use your entire THREE (3) UNIT BETTING STAKE against a SINGLE number. Win or lose, you DO have the edge. It is therefore an extra BONUS when you run into, and then parlay these Live Crap Rolls. These parlays on crap rolls are also our best way of overcoming Naturals (7s or 11s) that we BACKLINE BILLIES must put up with.

(4) Should the shooter roll a point (4-5-6-8-9-10), we would Lay Bet the odds. We now make a Don't Come Bet of $5. Should the shooter roll a point, other than the Don't Pass Line Point, we would Lay Bet the Odds, and make ONE MORE Don't Come bet. Should we again cover an open point, we would Lay Bet the Odds and our betting on this shooter is now completed.

77

(5) Should the shooter come out on a Pass Line Point, when betting the Don't Pass Line, and on his first Don't Come Line bet, repeat or BUCK the Pass Line Point, you would NOT make a third bet against this shooter. Here is what could happen:

(a) You could also lose the Don't Come Bet, and must now try to win enough on following shooters with your ONE remaining Unit to get back into a winning position.

(b) You could win the Don't Come bet, but still be a loser on your Betting Stake. (Providing of course that both bets are approximately the same size.) In this case, we wait for a NEW shooter and since we are a loser on our Betting Stake, we now bet $10 instead of $5 on the Don't Pass Line. Should we come out on a Natural (7-11), we would fold our arms and again wait for a new shooter. Should we come out on a point, we would Lay Bet the Odds, and if we still had part of a bet remaining, we would bet it on the Don't Come Line.

(c) We at all times keep a count of our THREE (3) UNIT INDIVIDUAL BETTING STAKE. Should we on a completed bet find we have more than $70, we take down and LOCK UP the difference. We start again with the initial $5 bet on the Don't Pass Line. (The amount over the $70 could be from $1 and up, but it must be over the $70.)

(6) After our TOTAL BETTING STAKE of $420 is used up, we count our lock-up chips. Should we find that we've shown a profit of ANY amount, but not enough to move up to our NEXT HIGHER betting level, we remain at the SAME table and start over again with the same sized Betting Stake. We pocket or cash in the profit.

Should we find that we have enough in our lock-up to move up to the next higher level, we do so and pocket or cash in any extra winnings. (Naturally we remain at the same table.)

Our next higher Total Betting Stake is $588, comprised of SIX (6) INDIVIDUAL BETTING STAKES OF $98 EACH. The increased FLAT PORTION of your starting bet is now $7 plus LAY BETTING DOUBLE ODDS. We NEVER move up more than one level at time.

(7) Should we find that we have taken a LOSS on our $420 Betting Stake, we would (if we wanted to continue playing) move on to the next CONSECUTIVELY NUMBERED table and start over again with another $420 Betting Stake. If we are at a floating crap game or a one table casino, we would of course continue at the same table.

THE MRS. DICE DOCTOR'S WRONG BETTING PLAY

In March of 1983, my wife Anne and I celebrated our 40th wedding anniversary. The following is the play that I've dedicated to her. (Although I have personally used this play since 1958, it is the first time that I've ever put a name to it, or put it in print.) . . . THE MRS. DICE DOCTOR'S PLAY.

This play contains parts of ALL the successful Wrong Betting moves that I've used since the early thirties. Many practicing crapshooters have the mistaken impression that Craps must be complicated in order to be successful. Nothing could be further from the truth. Without the laying of odds, this play has had a Winning Average of about 60%. With the laying of odds, 70%. I have personally used DOUBLE ODDS, and in the past few years, TRIPLE ODDS or better, wherever possible. The STOP LOSS moves makes it worth the extra investment required. The first example will be the using of FLAT BETS ONLY.

I found that 18 betting units, broken into six sets of three individual bets, gives your GAMBLING MONEY a FAIR GAMBLE. The 18 Units may be $1 chips, $5 chips, $25 chips, or any multiples of 18 that your TOTAL GAMBLING BANKROLL WARRANTS. Using a $90 BETTING STAKE, consisting of 18 Individual Betting Units of $5 each, we do the following: We place the $90 Betting Stake into the FRONT or BETTING PORTION of the CHECK RACK. The REAR or LOCK-UP PORTION will be used for any WINNING BETS.

(1) We bet $5 on the Don't Pass Line. The shooter rolls a Natural (7-11). This is our STOP LOSS MOVE on any Come-out Roll for either a Don't Pass Line or a Don't Come Line Point. We make no further bets against THIS shooter. (Till the next time around. Not forever!!) My number one rule for any Wrong Betting play is that YOU NEVER CHASE A LOSING BET. We now fold our arms and wait for the NEXT shooter to get the dice before we make our next bet.

(2) We bet $5 on the Don't Pass Line and the shooter rolls a LIVE or PAYOFF CRAPS. (1-1 or 1-2 where these pay off. 6-6 or 1-2 where THESE pay off.) We PARLAY or let ride the $10. We continue parlaying any number of CONSECUTIVE live or payoff craps, until the shooter establishes a Pass Line Point.

My personal record (until now) has been five (5) consecutive live or payoff Crap Rolls, before the shooter rolled his Pass Line Point of 8. He did not make the 8 and I received a payoff of $640 for the COMPLETED PARLAY. (I was at the time using $10 Betting Units.) I had before and have since, run into parlays of 5 consecutive crap rolls, only to have the shooter knock me off with a NATURAL (7-11) on the 6th roll, or else establish a Pass Line Point on the 6th roll and then proceed to make the point.

(3) We make a $5 bet on the Don't Pass Line. The shooter rolls a BAR POINT of 12 or two sixes. (Or two aces where they are the BAR POINT.) We do NOT get paid on this Bar or Stand-off roll. We pick up our bet on the Don't Pass Line (or the Don't Come Line) and wait for the NEXT shooter. (There is nothing as disappointing to the Wrong Bettor, than to bet on a 35 to 1 Craps Roll (the Bar Point) and not even get EVEN MONEY!!)

Yes, I know that without the Bar Point in Bank Craps (like casino or floating crap games) that the Wrong Bettors would have a BIG edge over the Right Bettors as they do in Army or Fade crap games where they don't use a Bar Point. The Bar Point at casino or floating Bank Craps, brings the House Edge to almost EQUAL against both the Right and the Wrong Bettor. (1.414 against the Right Bettor versus 1.402 against the Wrong Bettor.)

One other move concerning the Bar Point. Should the shooter have rolled one or more Live or Payoff Craps, and then roll a Bar Point, we would still take off the entire parlayed bet that we had going on the Don't Pass Line or the Don't Come Line. We would lock up any profit, and again wait for a NEW shooter to get the dice.

(4) We make a $5 bet on the Don't Pass Line. The shooter rolls a 6 or 8. We make NO further bets against THIS shooter. Should we win our bet, we would place the winning $5 into the REAR or LOCK-UP PORTION of the Chip Rack.

(5) We make a $5 bet on the Don't Pass Line and the shooter rolls a 5 or 9 for his Pass Line Point. (The 5 or 9 as a Pass Line Point permits us to make ONE bet on the Don't Come Line, for a total of 2 bets.) We now make a $5 bet on the Don't Come Line. The shooter rolls a 7 and we lose our Don't Come bet. We win our Don't Pass Line Bet, but this just leaves us EVEN. Since we are not at the Crap Game to BREAK EVEN, our bet on the next shooter is $10 on the Don't Pass Line. Should we win this bet, we would place the winning $10 into the Lock-up Rack and start over again on the next shooter with our normal $5 bet. Should we have lost this $10 bet on the Don't Pass Line, we would not replace it with $10 from our Rear or Lock-up portion of the Chip Rack. We as gamblers accept the loss and continue on the next shooter.

(6) We make a $5 bet on the Don't Pass Line, and the shooter rolls a 4 or 10. (When the Pass Line Point is 4 or 10, we may make TWO (2) bets on the Don't Come Line for a total of 3 bets. Unless we run into a STOP LOSS MOVE before the 3 bets are completed.)

We now make a $5 bet on the Don't Come Line, and the shooter rolls a number. (Different than the Don't Pass Line Number.) We now make another $5 bet on the Don't Come Line and the shooter rolls an eleven (11). We lose this Don't Come Line bet. We win our other 2 bets when the shooter sevens out. We receive a total payoff of $20 for a NET PROFIT of $5. We place the $5 profit into the Lock-up Portion of the Chip Rack.

Had the shooter made one of the two remaining bets we had covered, and we won the one bet, we would have to take the $10 we received and bet the entire $10 on the Don't Pass Line against the next shooter.

(7) On the LAST BET remaining in the Betting Stake, we may if necessary, take enough from our lock-up chips to properly complete that ONE bet.

(8) When you have made your last bet, count yuour LOCK-UP CHIPS. Should you find that you have shown a profit on your $90 Betting Stake, remain at the same table and start over again with your $90 Betting Stake. Pocket or cash in any winnings.

(9) At the end of a day's gambling session, take a count of your TOTAL GAMBLING BANKROLL. The next time you go to the crap tables, make your Betting Stake in accordance with your NEW Total Gambling Bankroll. If you are an occasional crapshooter, then 5% for any one Betting Stake is about right. If you gamble regularly or professionally, 1 or 2% of your Total Gambling Bankroll is enough for your Betting Stake.

(10) Simply put (aside from the STOP LOSS MOVES) when a 6 or 8 becomes the Pass Line Point, you do not make any further bets. ONE BET ONLY!

When a 5 or a 9 becomes the Pass Line Point, you would make ONE bet on the Don't Come Line. For a total of TWO (2) BETS.

When the 4 or 10 becomes the Pass Line Point, you would make TWO bets on the Don't Come Line. For a total of THREE (3) BETS.

LAYING ODDS IN THE MRS. DICE DOCTOR PLAY

I've claimed that even WITHOUT the laying of odds, this method of play is strong. You can therefore accept that the laying of SINGLE or MULTIPLE ODDS has an added advantage.

For example: without laying any odds, should you have your Don't Pass Line bet behind a number and then have the shooter seven out on the Don't Come Line bet, you would BREAK EVEN.

Now with the SAME BET, using Single or Multiple Odds (double, triple or better), you would have a FULL BET behind the Don't Pass Line number, and you would only lose a PART BET on the Don't Come Line seven-out. This would at least give you a NET PROFIT of a PART BET.

The Wrong Bettor will occasionally run into a string of POINT SEVENS. Without laying the odds, he would have to win TWO consecutive bets to show a NET PROFIT. On the using of Single or Multiple Odds, he gets a net profit on winning ONE BET.

Using SINGLE ODDS the $5 Bettor would require a $228 Betting Stake. The $25 Bettor would require a $1140 Betting Stake. Depending on your personal TOTAL GAMBLING BANKROLL you may figure out your own Betting Stake.

Laying DOUBLE ODDS the $5 Bettor would require a $348 Betting Stake. The $25 Bettor would require a $1740 Betting Stake.

Keep in mind the first cardinal rule for the successful Wrong Bettor, YOU NEVER CHASE A LOSING BET . . .

DOWNTOWN VEGAS BANKROLL	ATLANTIC CITY BANKROLL	FLAT BET BANKROLL
$1 Single $46.50	$2 Double $150	$1 No odds $18
$1 Double $75.00	$3 Single $162	$3 No odds $54
$2 Single $93.00	$3 Double $252	$5 No odds $90
	$5 Single $228	$25 No odds $450
	$5 Double $348	
	$25 Single $1140	
	$25 Double $1740